DETROIT PUBLIC LIBRARY

3 5674 00276117 0

W9-CBC-243

Understanding
Supreme
Court
Opinions

Understanding
Supreme Court Opinions

T. R. van Geel
University of Rochester

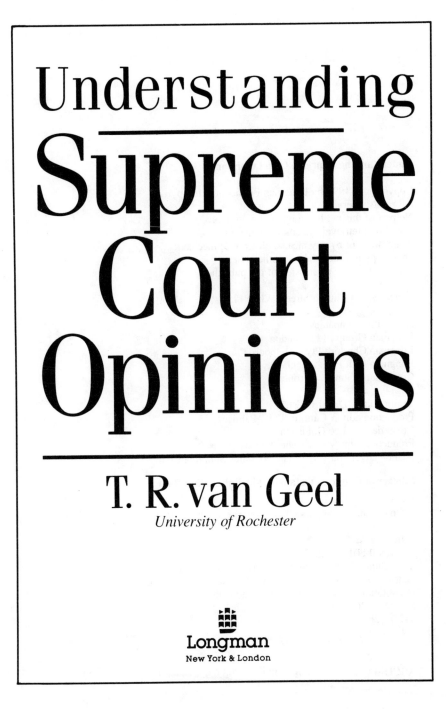

Longman
New York & London

REFERENCE

R347.7326
V293u

c.1

Understanding Supreme Court Opinions

Copyright © 1991 by Longman Publishing Group
All rights reserved.
No part of this publication may be reproduced,
stored in a retrieval system, or transmitted
in any form or by any means, electronic, mechanical,
photocopying, recording, or otherwise,
without the prior permission of the publisher.

Longman, 95 Church Street, White Plains, N.Y. 10601

Associated companies:
Longman Group Ltd., London
Longman Cheshire Pty., Melbourne
Longman Paul Pty., Auckland
Copp Clark Pitman, Toronto

Senior editor: David J. Estrin
Production editor: Camilla T. K. Palmer
Cover design: Lee Goldstein
Production supervisor: Anne Armeny
Seal on cover courtesy of United States Supreme Court

Library of Congress Cataloging-in-Publication Data

Van Geel, Tyll.
   Understanding Supreme Court opinions / by T. R. van Geel.
      p. cm.
   Includes index.
   ISBN 0-8013-0308-7
   1. United States Supreme Court.   2. Judicial process—United
States.   3. Judicial opinions—United States.   4. United States—
Constitutional law—Interpretation and construction.   I. Title.
KF8742.V36   1991
347.73'26—dc20
[347.30735]
                                                    90-6229
                                                    CIP

ABCDEFGHIJ—MU—99 98 97 96 95 94 93 92 91 90

For my parents, Ellinor and Pol van Geel,
with much love and appreciation

Contents

Preface

This book provides an introduction to the legal reasoning and the modes of persuasion and justification used by Supreme Court justices, as well as others engaged in constitutional adjudication. It attempts to provide a new perspective on the workings of the Supreme Court, thus also seeks to shed new light on the workings of our constitutional system and enrich our understanding of the notion of the rule of law.

The book is intended to be used in several ways. It is designed to be used as a supplement to a constitutional law casebook, as well as a book that can be combined with other materials written from the perspective of the political scientist.

The idea for this book grew out of my experiences in teaching an undergraduate constitutional law course at the University of Rochester. Among the goals I had established for this course were simultaneously introducing students to the substance of constitutional law and introducing them to the methods of reasoning and analysis used in constitutional law. But the problem I faced was that it was difficult to achieve these goals in one semester when students brought with them little or no legal background. Thus I cast around for a way to make more efficient and effective the learning of constitutional reasoning and analysis. I wanted to improve the course so that students themselves would earlier in the semester begin to learn to use analytical and reasoning skills that the Supreme Court justices used in writing the opinions assigned in the course. This would help students both become more astute readers of those opinions and improve their abilities to work with those opinions to address novel constitutional issues.

There are a number of books on the market that discuss legal methodology and reasoning generally, but I found no book that specifically addressed constitutional reasoning as practiced by the United States Supreme Court. I therefore turned to the writing of my own introduction, which at first took the form of a long paper which I placed on reserve in the library. Over a period of four years I revised the paper, and it is from that paper that this book grew.

There are thus literally hundreds of University of Rochester students to whom I am indebted for giving me the opportunity to teach and who demonstrated such an enormous interest in constitutional law that they fed my desire to be an ever better teacher for them. I especially want to acknowledge the help of the following who volunteered to read and comment on the first drafts of the completed book: Luke Bellocchi, Robert Hughes, Scott Glotzer, Douglas Gerhardt, Jon Getz, Dan Minich, and David Mustard. I alwo owe much thanks to Alexandra van Geel for her comments on several chapters. To Professor Martha McMarthy and Steven E. Gottlieb I want to say thanks for your support and insightful comments and suggestions. Finally, there is somewhere in this land an anonymous, to me, reader of this manuscript whose detailed and conscientiously developed critique of two versions of the book did much to improve it. The weaknesses that remain are certainly my responsibility, but I am grateful for the suggestions and the willingness to share and collaborate.

Introduction

Some years ago when I was in college, and about to go on to law school, I had a conversation with a lawyer in my home town. He told me that I would enjoy law school if I enjoyed reading lots of "little stories." Well, in law school I did read lots of little stories, but it was also clear that what that lawyer had told me was misleading. It was true that the judicial opinions I read were stories with considerable human conflict, drama, and passion. But by calling these accounts "little stories" he had intimated that these stories were not complex and intricate. He seemed to suggest that they were no more than a series of interesting anecdotes. In fact, each was more like a Shakespearian play with multiple characters, a complex structure, densely packed language, and several layers of meaning. These were not mere tabloid accounts of human conflict but rich pieces of writing that even with multiple readings yielded new insights.

While the reading and understanding of law is often compared to the reading and understanding of literature, let me suggest a different comparison. You are an historian of ancient Rome, and you are working with the speeches of a famous Roman senator delivered in the Roman senate. In trying to understand the meaning and significance of these speeches you will be asking yourself these and other questions:

- What social function did the giving of speeches serve? Why did this senator and other senators give speeches? What role did the Roman senate have in the system of government?
- On what occasion was this speech given? Who was the audience?
- Under what constraints did a senator operate when delivering a speech?

Were there things that Roman senators could not say or were expected to say?

- What was the logical argument of the speech? What point was it making and how did it justify that point?
- What materials did the speech rely on to make its point?
- Were the assumptions and premises of the speech plausible at that historical moment in time? Are they still plausible today?
- How does this speech compare with previous speeches given by the same senator? other senators? Are there different styles of speeches?
- What underlying values and beliefs were embodied in the speech?
- What were the political, economic, and social effects of this speech?

The questions you may wish to ask about the speeches of the Roman senate are in many respects the same questions one should be asking about the opinions of the United States Supreme Court. As was true of the speeches of the Roman senators, the opinions of Supreme Court justices are written within a particular institutional setting and are designed to serve certain social, political, and, of course, legal functions. A judicial opinion must be understood in light of the institutional setting in which it was written. Not the least of these functions is that these opinions are intended to be *persuasive* arguments. The opinion is designed to convince the reader that the judgment reached in the case—the bottom line— was correct.

You need to understand all this as well as why this particular opinion was being delivered at this time. How did it come to be that the Supreme Court rendered this opinion at this point?

To understand the opinion one needs to realize that the justices operate under a variety of legal, political, and social constraints and expectations. These limitations force the opinion-writer to write in a certain style, to use only certain kinds of materials to support his or her arguments. These constraints and expectations have an important effect on the tone, the voice, and the style of the opinion. It is these constraints and expectations which force the opinion to sound and look like a *legal* opinion and not just, for example, the expression of a political opinion.

Beyond trying to understand the social and political function of opinions in general, one must also get into the content of the opinions. What was its point? What were the arguments made in support of that point? Were the premises of those arguments well supported? What are its unspoken values, assumptions, and principles? And what was the political, economic, and social effect of the opinion?

Clearly, reading and understanding Supreme Court opinions involves something more than reading little stories. And this book is designed to help in the learning of the skills needed to come to a full understanding of these documents which have such a special place in our legal and political system. To that end

Chapter 1 provides background information essential to understanding those opinions. This chapter discusses the Constitution itself and the Supreme Court's role in interpreting and enforcing the United States Constitution. The chapter also talks about how cases or problems get to the Supreme Court, and how it comes to be that the Court issues its opinions.

In the course of reviewing constitutional law in Chapter 1, I will introduce a theme that will become more prominent in Chapter 2, the task of writing a Supreme Court opinion as seen from the perspective of a justice on the Supreme Court. Thus, Chapter 2 discusses the constraints and expectations a justice faces in the writing of opinions. My belief is that one can become a better reader or consumer of Supreme Court opinions if one can appreciate the writing of those opinions from the perspective of a justice.

Chapters 3, 4, and 5 are an introduction to how the justices have handled three important aspects of judicial opinion writing. Chapter 3 discusses three basic *strategies of justification* that the justices have used in writing opinions. A strategy of justification is the general approach an opinion can take to accomplish its task of persuading a reader of the correctness of the Court's judgment. To take one example, the opinion may use the strategy of justification called the *analogy*: (1) This case is like previous case "A." (2) Like cases ought to be treated alike. (3) In the previous case we did "X." (4) Therefore, in this case we shall also do "X."

This, and the other two strategies of justification, are not by themselves sufficient to write an opinion. They are like carpenter's tools; that is, necessary implements to build a house but not sufficient. To complete the structure one still needs building materials. Thus, in Chapter 4, I turn to a discussion of the building materials a justice must work with in constructing an opinion. These materials include, among other things, the text of the Constitution itself, evidence of the intent of the framers, evidence of contemporary moral values, and precedent. Unfortunately, there are many controversies and problems surrounding the use of these and other legal materials; this chapter introduces these disuptes.

One of the most important building materials the justices must use in constructing a persuasive opinion is precedent; that is, prior Supreme Court opinions. But, again, there are many problems surrounding the use of precedent. Chapter 5 provides an introduction to these problems as well as a perspective on how the justices have used (and abused) precedent. You will learn that working with precedent, as is true of working with the other construction materials discussed in Chapter 4, takes skill and art. These materials can be used in a variety of ways, and knowing what these materials can and cannot do is part of learning what it means to become an effective justice of the Supreme Court as well as an effective lawyer.

The concluding Chapter 6 brings the materials of the previous chapters together. A single Supreme Court opinion is reprinted and the chapter then proceeds to provide a detailed analysis of it. Just one caution: Each Supreme Court opinion is in important respects a unique document, different from other opinions. Thus, the kind of analysis one may undertake of one opinion will differ in some respects from the analysis of other opinions. But Chapter 6 should prepare one to get started in the interpretation and analysis of other opinions.

To conclude, an opinion is not a self-report of the internal decision-making processes of the Court itself or the internal mental deliberations of the individual justice who wrote the opinion. Opinions are documents designed to persuade, to convince the reader that the judgment the opinion reached was correct. That is to say, opinions are documents designed to serve legal, political and social functions. And when a justice approaches the writing of an opinion, he or she, typically, has several ways available in which the justification of the judgment can be written. The opinion writer thus can choose among different options in crafting the justification for the decision reached. Crafting the argument in such a way that it has the appearance of there having been no other way the opinion could have been written, and so convincing that it appears that no other decision could have been reached, is a high art form.

Viewing Supreme Court opinion writing as a high rhetorical form can make one cynical about the Supreme Court, the justices, lawyers, and law school training. Are judges and lawyers merely people with great rhetorical skills which they can use to justify any position they want to justify? Are law schools and courses in law vehicles for preparing people to be skilled rhetoricians? I believe the answer to these questions is in part "yes." But this is only a fraction of the story. It is also important that courts and judges reach wise decisions, sound decisions. It is important that lawyers consider seriously the cases they take, the kind of clients they represent, and the positions they advocate.

Thus it is important, vitally important, for the future of law and our society, that law schools and undergraduate courses in law be concerned not merely with preparing people to be rhetorically skilled. I believe teachers of law should wrestle in their courses with questions of right and justice. Students of the law should be concerned not only with developing analytical and rhetorical skills but also with formulating their own values and beliefs, their own views of right and justice. The following story illustrates my concern:

DEVIL SPEAKING TO AN ATTORNEY: I can give you riches beyond your wildest dreams. I can make you the most famous lawyer in all the land. You will win every case you undertake. The world will beat a path to your door. And in exchange for all this I will merely take your soul, the soul of your wife, and the souls of your children.

ATTORNEY: That's great! But what's the hitch?

CHAPTER 1

The Supreme Court and the Constitution

The United States Constitution is the supreme law of the land. Federal, state, and local governments, their legislative, judicial, and administrative branches, as well as all federal and state officials and employees, must conform their actions, policies, and laws to constitutional requirements (see Addendum to Chapter 1). Sometimes this is easily accomplished because the constitutional text is precise. Few would debate whether each state is to be represented by two senators. But other phrases and words of the Constitution are not so clear. For example, section 1 of Article II says that no person except a "natural born" citizen is eligible to be President. Presumably this means the President must have been born on American soil and not have obtained citizenship through naturalization procedures. But what of the person born on an American ship sailing in international waters? Does the phrase "natural born" exclude from the Presidency men and women born by means of caesarean section? These questions have not yet been officially answered, and the very fact we must ask them suggests that the constitutional text is not always clear.

A vague or ambiguous constitutional text is an obvious invitation to disputes over its meaning. In fact, disputes regularly arise between different branches of the federal government, between the federal government and the states, and between, on the one hand, federal or state government, and on the other hand, an individual. There thus arises the need for having some way to get a resolution of the dispute and an authoritative interpretation. Since 1803 the Supreme Court has played this role. In *Marbury v. Madison* (1803) the Court declared that the Constitution authorized it to determine when the challenged law or policy was inconsistent with the Constitution.

1

Because we, as a people, expect the Supreme Court to justify its exercise of this politically, economically, and socially important power of judicial review, the Court at the conclusion of many of its cases writes an opinion explaining and justifying the decision it reached. These opinions are precedent for the lower courts, and are used by lawyers to advise their clients (which include governmental officials) what it is they now believe is constitutionally permitted and what is constitutionally prohibited. It is these same opinions which form the basis of most courses in constitutional law. Unfortunately, these opinions, like the Constitution itself, are not free from vagueness and ambiguity; hence they, like the Constitution itself, require careful reading and interpretation.

The interpretation of Supreme Court opinions is a skill that needs to be learned. This chapter begins instruction in this skill by outlining in general terms the kinds of constitutional disputes the Supreme Court has been asked to resolve and the various roles the Court has played in our constitutional scheme. These sections also introduce some of the criteria the Court has used in deciding who is right in its interpretation of the Constitution. The next major section of the chapter takes up the question of how these disputes get to the Supreme Court and something about the internal decision-making process of the Court as it decides its cases. The last section introduces the Supreme Court opinion itself by outlining in general terms the major parts of the typical opinion.

CONSTITUTIONAL CONFLICTS

Constitutional conflicts involve fundamental issues of right and wrong; principles of social justice, power, and authority; oppression and liberty; economic development; and even war and security. But the language of right and wrong, liberty and justice is not the language in which the Supreme Court discusses these disputes. Take, for example, the issue of the minimum wage. In the legislature the question of whether a law should be passed requiring employers to pay a minimum wage may be debated in terms of the free market versus the welfare state, the protection of the working poor versus the loss of jobs. Once a minimum wage law has been passed and challenged as an unconstitutional exercise of legislative power, the terms of the debate shift to such questions as whether the law is a violation of the Fourteenth Amendment's prohibition against the deprivation of life, liberty, or property without due process of law.

The difference between the language of policy and constitutional language can be illustrated in a different way. Of central importance to American policy-makers is the problem of how to honor the principle of tolerance of antithetical political and cultural differences without going so far as to flirt with social disunity. The Supreme Court has played an important "navigator's" role in steering the ship of state on this course. But it has done so using language and concepts derived from the constitutional text. Thus the Court's opinions touching upon these issues have spoken in terms of such concepts as equal protection and the free exercise of religion.

Because Supreme Court opinions speak about fundamental issues of social policy in the language of the Constitution it is important to start toward an understanding of these opinions by looking at the Constitution itself.

AN OVERVIEW OF THE CONSTITUTION

The Constitution includes these five fundamental features:

- Provisions that touch upon such matters as the relationship between Congress, the President and the Supreme Court, their respective powers, and how the officers of these three branches are elected or appointed
- Provisions that regulate the relationship between, on the one hand, the federal government, and, on the other hand, the states
- Provisions designed to protect individuals against governmental invasions of their liberty, privacy, and other rights
- Provisions that guarantee persons the equal protection of the laws or otherwise prohibit invidious discrimination
- The two clauses of the First Amendment regulative of the relationship between government and religion

There are, of course, other provisions of the Constitution of great importance (e.g., section 3 of Article IV governing the admission of new states to the union, Article V which establishes the procedures for amending the Constitution, and Article VI which declares the Constitution the supreme law of the land). But the obtaining of a general understanding of the constitutional framework and the roles that the Supreme Court has played in interpreting those provisions can be addressed in terms of the five features listed above.

The conflicts which have arisen in each of the five areas all have one thing in common, namely, they begin with a dispute over what a government (federal, state, or local) or governmental official has done. The dispute may be brought to Court by another branch of government, a private person, or private business, but the genesis of the dispute must be in the official acts of a government, governmental official, or someone acting at the behest of a government. That is to say, constitutional conflicts are over what government or governmental officials (federal, state or local) have done or what government has gotten someone to do. These are not disputes solely between two private citizens, solely between a private citizen and a business, or solely between two businesses. Constitutional disputes are about governmental actions, or in the language of constitutional doctrine, about *state action*. Why is this the case? The answer is that the Constitution is a charter for *governmental* behavior, not a charter for regulating purely private relationships.

This is a reality of constitutional law that leads to some perhaps surprising conclusions. For example, if an employee is fired by a company for publicly criticizing that company's environmental record, this dismissal does not raise a constitutional free speech issue. Why? The reason is that the company is a private enterprise and its actions are not directly governed by the Constitution. But if that same employee were fired for the same reason by a local municipality, that dismissal would raise a constitutional issue of freedom of speech (*Pickering v. Board of Education* [1968]). The efforts of the National Collegiate Athletic Association to discipline a basketball coach for improprieties in his basketball program is an effort by a private organization and does not raise "constitutional" issues (*National Collegiate Athletic Association v. Tarkanian*, [1988]). Or take the case of the father who had been beating his infant son for two years; the last beating placed the boy in a life-threatening coma from which he emerged permanently brain damaged. Local officials were aware of the problem but took no steps to remove the boy from the father's care until it was too late. Does this raise a constitutional issue? "No," said the Supreme Court (*DeShaney v. Winnebago County Department of Social Services* [1989]). First, the father's abuse was the abuse by one private individual of another—the Constitution does not itself regulate this behavior. (State criminal law does.) Second, the failure of the local social services agency to act also was not a constitutional violation because the Constitution does not require government to protect the life, liberty, and property of its citizens. "The [Constitution] is phrased as a limitation on the State's power to act, not as a guarantee of certain minimum levels of safety and security."

THE COURT AS SUPERVISOR OF THE BOUNDARIES OF EXECUTIVE, LEGISLATIVE, AND JUDICIAL AUTHORITY (FIRST FEATURE)

Judicial Power

The Constitution establishes the three branches of the federal government and defines their respective powers. Because the grants of power to the three branches are phrased in general terms, disputes regularly arise regarding the scope of these grants. Take for example the problem of "judicial power." Article III of the Constitution gives the Supreme Court "judicial power." This general grant of power does not explicitly empower the Supreme Court to review the constitutionality of the statutes adopted by Congress and signed by the President. Thus one must turn to other materials to answer the question whether the notion of "judicial power" includes the power of "judicial review," the power to strike down as unconstitutional the acts of the other branches of government. The Supreme Court addressed this question in one of its earliest cases.

In *Marbury v. Madison* (1803), Chief Justice John Marshall wrote that the Supreme Court did have the power, even the duty, to review the constitutionality of the acts of Congress. The Chief Justice offered several justifications for the Court's exercise of this power, including the following:

1. The Constitution is a form of law. In fact, it is the supreme law of the land.
2. As the supreme law it also binds the Supreme Court.
3. When a federal statute conflicts with the Constitution, it is void.
4. When confronted with a case which involves a federal statute in conflict with the Constitution, the Court must determine which of these two laws is to be used in resolving the case before the Court—statute or Constitution.
5. Since the Constitution is superior to any ordinary law, the Court is duty bound to give force to the Constitution; to do otherwise would subvert the principle of a written constitution.

(Scholars have criticized this justification on the grounds that it begs the question of who is to determine what the Constitution means. While Marshall may be correct that the Court is duty bound to enforce the Constitution, that still does not answer the question whether the Court may willy-nilly adopt an interpretation of the Constitution different from that relied upon by the legislature.)

Having taken for itself the power of judicial review, the Court set itself up as an important arbiter of disputes regarding the scope of the authority of the President and Congress. Specifically in the *Marbury* case, the Court decided the question whether Congress constitutionally could expand the Supreme Court's "original" jurisdiction. The Constitution gives the Supreme Court two forms of jurisdiction, original and appellate jurisdiction. (Original jurisdiction exists when a court takes a case at its inception, tries it, and passes judgment. Appellate jurisdiction is the authority to take and review a case after it was decided by a court with original jurisdiction.) The Supreme Court's original jurisdiction is limited to a narrow class of cases, namely, cases affecting ambassadors, other public ministers and consuls, and those in which a state is a party to the case. One of the issues in the *Marbury* case was whether or not Congress had the authority to expand the Court's original jurisdiction to include a much broader class of cases. The Court said "no" and, using the power of judicial review, declared a federal statute which expanded the Court's own original jurisdiction to be unconstitutional.

Legislative Power

One of the most famous examples of the Supreme Court's defining congressional power came in *McCulloch v. Maryland* (1819). In that case the Court was asked to decide whether or not Congress had the authority to charter a national bank.

Article I's listing of the powers of Congress makes no express mention of such a power; thus the Court was forced to ask if bank chartering were an implied or inherent authority.

To begin answering this question, Chief Justice Marshall started by reviewing the other provisions of the constitutional text. He took note that Article I, Section 8 of the Constitution empowered Congress to "make all Law which shall be necessary and proper for carrying into Execution" both the specific powers granted to Congress and "all other Powers vested by this Constitution in the Government of the United States, or in any Department or Officer thereof." He also noted that the Constitution expressly granted Congress authority to lay and collect taxes, to borrow money, to regulate commerce, to declare and conduct war, and to raise and support armies and navies. He next suggested that it was in the interest of the nation to facilitate the execution of these powers, and that we have to presume that the framers intended to give to Congress the appropriate means to carry out these powers. He noted that the Constitution should not be read as a "splendid bauble." Thus, he argued, the "necessary and proper" clause authorized Congress to use any means calculated to produce the end. And, since chartering a bank is an appropriate means to the ends specifically mentioned in the Constitution, bank chartering should be viewed as power incidental to those powers which are expressly listed in the text.

Historically the Court has also played an important role in defining Congressional power to regulate interstate commerce. To understand these disputes I want to draw a distinction between two types of challenges. Constitutional challenges that claim, for example, that the term "legislative power" does not include the power to charter a bank raise an "internal" question of power (i.e., a question of the definition of the term "legislative power"). But Congress may have the legislative power to carry out a specific act, given the definition of the term "legislative power," but the exercise of this power may, nevertheless, transgress an "external" check on the power. Such an external check might be a constitutional right of an individual, the authority of another branch of the federal government to deal with the matter, or the sovereignty of a state.

Article I expressly authorizes Congress to regulate "interstate commerce," but serious questions exist regarding the scope of that power and, especially, whether "external" limits are imposed upon that authority by the separate existence and sovereignty of the states. Consider, for example, the following issues with which the Court had to deal: May Congress prohibit the transportation across state lines of lottery tickets? (Yes.) May Congress regulate labor practices in the steel industry on the grounds that intrastate labor disputes affect interstate commerce? (Yes.) May Congress control the amount of wheat a farmer grows solely for his family's private consumption, that is, wheat that will not enter the flow of interstate commerce? (Yes.) May Congress, pursuant to its power to regulate interstate commerce, prohibit a small family-owned barbecue, serving a local clientele, from refusing to serve customers on the basis of race? (Yes, again.)

In rendering these decisions the Court considered the text of the Constitution (the meaning of the phrase "interstate commerce"); the principle of federalism and the concurrent authority of states to regulate these same activities; the intent of the framers; precedent; and practical considerations such as the desirability of a sound national economy. It was in terms of these legal materials that the Court forged its justifications for its expansive interpretation of Congress's authority.

The Court has used these same legal materials in considering other issues of Congressional power, such as the scope of Congress's authority to tax and spend (Article I, Section 8). Again the express words of the text do not provide a definitive answer to the question whether Congress may "coerce" states or individuals to take certain actions, or adopt certain policies, by using federal funds as a carrot. For example, the issue arose whether Congress may withhold federal highway funds from those states which permit individuals under twenty-one to purchase or possess in public any alcoholic beverage. (The answer is "yes" (*South Dakota v. Dole* [1987].) In justifying its answer the Court made reference to the text of the Constitution, the debate between James Madison and Alexander Hamilton over the meaning of the general welfare clause, the definition of the concept of "coercion," and the principle of federalism.

Presidential Power

Just as the Court has demarked the boundaries of congressional authority it has also done important work in defining the power of the President. One famous occasion of the Court's exercise of this responsibility arose when President Truman directed the Secretary of Commerce to seize the operation of the nation's steelmills during wartime. The President issued this directive in the face of a strike by steelworkers that threatened to interrupt the flow of steel necessary for the war effort. Significant to the case was the fact that the President acted without any authorization from Congress; he simply relied on the Constitution's general grant of executive authority (*Youngstown Sheet & Tube Co. v. Sawyer* [1952]). To answer the question whether the President had the authority to commandeer the steelmills the justices asked: (1) whether the power had been expressly granted by the Constitution, (2) whether the power may be implied from the Constitutional text, (3) whether or not the power was an inherent power of the President.

The Court began its analysis by turning to the constitutional text itself, but it found no express authorization for such an order. The justices next examined the concept of "executive power" and the role of the President in our constitutional scheme of government in an attempt to answer questions (2) and (3). Even assuming the justices had concluded that the President had the authority to issue such an order (they, in fact, did not so conclude), they would still have had to ask whether the President's authority was limited by considerations "external" to the grant of power to him. These "external" checks on the President's power include: (1) a constitutional grant of authority over the same topic to Congress (e.g., Congress's authority to declare and make war), and (2) the separate existence and "sovereignty" of the states. That is to say, the scope of presidential power must be reconciled with the grants of authority to Congress and the states, grants which may authorize them to deal with the same subject matter.

Separation of Powers

A brief glance at the Constitution reveals that the *legislative* branch has been given neither "judicial" nor "executive" power, that the judicial branch enjoys neither legislative nor executive power, and that the executive branch has neither legislative nor judicial power. Yet, at the same time, the Constitution often requires the cooperation of two branches of government (e.g., Congress has the power to declare war, but the President is the commander in chief).

The complexity of this arrangement, the interdependence of the branches, has led to continuing competition and conflict among the federal branches—conflicts that can threaten their independence and integrity. Thus it often falls to the Court to umpire among the three branches, even when its own integrity is at stake. Consider, for example, the case of *United States v. Nixon* (1974).

In that case several former aides and advisers to President Nixon were under criminal indictment and the court in which they were being tried issued a subpoena to President Nixon ordering him to produce certain tape recordings and documents concerning his conversations with his aides and advisers. The President claimed that the principle of "executive privilege"—the notion that the President may withhold information from the other branches of government—justified his request to quash the subpoena. The lower court refused to quash the subpoena, and the President appealed to the Supreme Court. The principle of separation of powers figured into (1) the question of whether the Supreme Court could review the President's claim of the privilege; (2) whether there was an absolute and unqualified executive privilege; and (3) if there were only a qualified executive privilege, when that claim might be overridden.

The Supreme Court in *United States v. Nixon* concluded there was only a "qualified privilege," and that in this instance the privilege could not be invoked (the Court refused to quash the subpoena). The Court concluded that there was a "qualified privilege" despite the fact that the notion of executive privilege was not expressly mentioned in the Constitution itself.

The Court justified its conclusion that there was a qualified privilege by arguing that it was implied by a tacit principle embedded in the constitutional structure—the principle of the separation of powers. The integrity of the Presidency, said the Court, required the existence of such a privilege. But the Court also concluded that the integrity of the judicial branch, the need for a fair criminal trial, required that the qualified privilege be denied in this case. To justify this conclusion the Court's opinion mounted a pragmatic argument: To allow the privilege in this instance would do more harm to the judiciary than provide benefits to the Presidency; the harm done to the Presidency by not recognizing the claim to executive privilege in this case was offset by the benefits of protecting the integrity of the judicial system and the public's belief in the possibility of obtaining a fair trial in the nation's judicial system.

The *Nixon* case represents only one way in which the separation of powers principle comes into play. Perhaps more typical are the disputes which arise when Congress attempts to carry out a social policy by setting up institutional structures which commingle the functions of the branches of the federal government. For example, the delegation by Congress to an officer in the executive branch or a judge in the judicial branch of certain "legislative" powers raises the issue of the separation of powers (*Mistretta v. United States* [1989], *Bowsher v. Synar* [1986]).

THE COURT AS UMPIRE OF FEDERAL-STATE RELATIONS (SECOND FEATURE)

Federalism and the Federal Government's Control of the States

The Supreme Court has been called upon not only to resolve disputes among the three branches of the federal government but also to supervise the relationship between those three branches, on the one hand, and the states, on the other. This role has led the Court to consider questions of federal power touching upon the following:

- Direct federal regulation of the operations of state and local government
- Federal taxation of state and local activities
- Federal regulation of an activity which preempts state efforts to regulate that same activity

Behind each of these problems lies the general question of whether Congress may regulate the states themselves as states. Relevant to answering this question is the principle of federalism acknowledging that the states have separate and independent existence that is to be preserved as a check against excessive centralized power.

Let's look at two related examples of the Court's work in this area. In *National League of Cities v. Usery* (1976) the Court concluded that Congress improperly invaded the sovereign and independent status of the states when it undertook to prescribe a minimum wage for state and local public employees. A minimum wage law imposed on state and local operations, said the Court, impaired an indisputable attribute of state sovereignty and a function which had been traditionally a function of state and local government. Only nine years later, in *Garcia v. San Antonio Metropolitan Transit Authority* (1985), the Court reconsidered this conclusion and ruled that Congress did have this authority. The Court stated that its experience with the rule from *Usery* showed that its rule was unworkable. Over the years the Court had been unable to define in a consistent way which local functions were protected from Congressional control and which were not. And the Court relied on its newer understanding of the intent of the framers. In *Garcia* the majority said that the framers intended to have the sovereignty of the states protected through the political process rather than by the Court. That is to say, because states as states had representation in the Senate, those representatives could themselves guard against overreaching by the federal government.

Federalism and State Control of Federal Operations

Not only has the Court been asked to supervise federal control of the states, it has also been called upon to examine the scope of *state* authority.

- State taxation of the operations of the federal government
- State regulation and taxation of interstate commerce, activities the federal government is expressly authorized to regulate
- State discrimination—barriers and obstacles—against goods and services in interstate commerce coming from other states in order to protect local industries

If left unchecked these state activities would lead to severe frustration of the federal government and the balkanization and weakening of the national economy. Thus, over the years the Court has played the important role of defining and limiting state power to prevent these damaging consequences.

Take, for example, state regulation of interstate transportation. The Court's opinions typically begin by noting that Congress has been expressly granted authority to regulate interstate commerce. This grant of authority to Congress the Court interprets as operating as an external limitation on the concurrent power of the states to regulate interstate commerce. That is, the Court has said that the grant of authority to Congress to regulate interstate commerce, even if the Congress has not used its power and it lies dormant, is relevant to understanding the scope of the *states'* authority to regulate interstate commerce.

Using this approach the Court has fashioned, over the years, different ways for gauging the legitimate scope of state authority. At one point in the Court's history it said that state authority to regulate depended on whether the impact of the state's regulation on interstate commerce was "direct" or "indirect." Today the Court justifies its conclusions in terms of balancing several considerations (*Pike v. Bruce Church, Inc.* [1970]):

> Where the statute regulates evenhandedly to effectuate a legitimate local public interest, and its effects on interstate commerce are only incidental, it will be upheld unless the burden imposed on such commerce is clearly excessive in

relation to the putative local benefits. If a legitimate local purpose is found, then the question becomes one of degree. And the extent of the burden that will be tolerated will of course depend on the nature of the local interest involved, and on whether it could be promoted as well with a lesser impact on interstate activities.

Thus an opinion involving the "dormant commerce clause" will set forth and then "apply" this test to the facts of the case. The discussion applying the test will constitute a major portion of the opinion leading up to the conclusion. And the judgment regarding the constitutionality of the state policy will be justified in terms of whether or not the state regulation satisfied or failed this "test."

INTERLUDE: TESTS AND STANDARDS OF REVIEW, A FIRST LOOK

Supreme Court opinions addressing questions regarding the grant of authority are typically structured around these issues: Is this an express, implied, or inherent power? Is this power checked or limited by the existence of another grant of authority (e.g., by a grant to another branch of the federal government, by state sovereignty, by the "dormant commerce clause")? The justifications reached in these cases are phrased in terms of an analysis of the text of the Constitution, intent of the framers, the principles of separation of powers and federalism, precedent, and the practical consequences of recognizing or denying the existence of the power.

Let's now look more closely at the notion of a "test" as introduced in connection with the discussion of state regulation of interstate commerce. As will be discussed in Chapter 2, Supreme Court justices work under an obligation to write their opinions in such a way that those opinions provide guidance for the future (i.e., guidance in helping us predict what judgment the Court will reach in other cases involving similar problems). One way to help provide this guidance, and at the same time give the appearance the opinion is based on general principles of law applied in a dispassionate, objective, and neutral way, is to develop and rely upon "tests" and "standards of review." (I use the terms "test" and "standard of review" interchangeably.) These tests are verbal formulas which set forth the requirements a law, policy, or action must satisfy if it is to be upheld. Thus the example quoted above indicates, roughly speaking, that if a state law regulating interstate transportation is to be upheld it must (1) regulate evenhandedly (not discriminate against out of state commerce); (2) serve a legitimate local public purpose (e.g., not be designed to promote racial segregation); (3) have only an incidental impact on interstate commerce (its effect must be slight); and (4) the burden on interstate commerce must not be excessive in relation to the local benefits (the local benefits must outweigh the harm done to interstate commerce).

The use of this test, or any test, can involve many complex problems—determining the degree of impact the regulation has, weighing the benefits of the regulation against the harm done to interstate commerce. But the *logic* involved in using these tests is straightforward: (1) To be constitutional the state law must satisfy test "A." (2) This law does (or does not) satisfy the test. (3) Therefore, the law is (un)constitutional. A carefully crafted justification will develop and support premises (1) and (2), using the appropriate legal materials and factual findings.

There are literally dozens of such tests in constitutional law. Let's look at one more example. In the opinion dealing with whether or not Congress had the authority to establish a national bank, Chief Justice Marshall promulgated the following test of the scope of Congress's authority: "Let the end be legitimate, let it be within the scope of the constitution, and all means which are appropriate, which are plainly adapted to that end, which are not prohibited, but consistent with the letter and spirit of the constitution, are constitutional." This test is still cited today by the Court in cases involving challenges to Congress's authority. Different tests come into play in connection with such constitutional problems as Congress's authority to regulate interstate commerce and Congress's taxing and spending power.

There are several things about these tests that you should note. These tests are not to be found in the Constitution itself. The tests are judicial creations and the Court with fair regularity has changed, modified, reinterpreted, and discarded tests. Arguments over the derivation and choice of a test, as well as the interpretation and application of a test, are one vehicle (rhetorical mode) judges use to express their disagreements. Majority and dissenting opinions often reflect disagreements about the selection of a test or the interpretation of a test. Justice Scalia, for example, is today engaged in efforts to get the other members of the Court to abandon the test announced in the *Pike* case which the Court has used to determine the constitutionality of state regulations of business which affect interstate commerce (*Tyler Pipe Industries, Inc. v. Washington Dep't. of Revenue* [1987]; *Goldberg v. Sweet* [1989]). And the lawyers representing opposing parties may also disagree over which is the appropriate test to be used, or how to interpret and apply a particular test. (Chapter 5 further discusses the interpretation of precedent and tests.)

SUPERVISING GOVERNMENT'S RELATIONSHIP WITH THE INDIVIDUAL (THIRD FEATURE)

One of the Court's most visible activities is its role in supervising the relationship between government (all federal, state, and local branches) and the individual. It carries out this function by discovering, recognizing, defining, and protecting the constitutional rights of individuals. The significance of these rights is that they operate as an "external" restraint on the power of all levels of government. The individual right is, thus, a shield against certain governmental actions. It, in some instances, provides the person with a guaranteed liberty that he or she may do something—give a speech—free from governmental interference. Hence, generally speaking, the individual rights protected by the Constitution are of the so-called "negative" variety—rights which impose a duty on government *not* to do something. Except, arguably, in the criminal area where government must, among other things, provide a fair trial, these rights do not impose a duty on government to take affirmative steps to do something. For example, the Court has not interpreted the Constitution to require government to guarantee the poor a minimum level of income or even minimum levels of safety and security. Welfare programs may voluntarily be undertaken by government, and, having undertaken such a program, the government is under the negative duty not to operate the program in a, for example, racially discriminatory manner. But the Constitution today is not understood to require government to establish a social safety net.

Some constitutional rights are treated as if they were absolute (e.g., the right of a criminal defendant to a lawyer). This means that if the right exists, a violation of it cannot be justified, or excused, by a claimed overriding public interest. The right operates as a kind of trump card which overrides claims that in this one instance the right should give way because of an important governmental interest. Any accommodation with important governmental interests must be accomplished by either defining the right narrowly or creating exceptions to it (e.g., yes, you have a right to a lawyer, except when you are making your second appeal of the same criminal conviction).

Outside the criminal field, people talk about rights differently. The rights tend to be broadly defined (e.g., the right to freedom of speech). But these rights are not treated as absolute. Instead their violation may be justified in certain instances when government may have sufficient reason to infringe them. For example, you may have a general right of freedom of speech, but the governmental interest in preventing panic in theaters is so strong that, if you were to yell fire in the theater, the government could punish you for doing so. This too broad statement rides roughshod over many important distinctions in constitutional law, but it serves as a useful starting point for our purposes. As you learn more about constitutional law, you will better understand the criticisms that can be made of the distinction drawn here and the somewhat inaccurate manner in which the "absolute" and "nonabsolute" cases are described.

As arbiter of the relationship between government and individuals through the mechanism of the individual right, the Court typically must go through a series of steps in defining the relationship. The first three steps listed below are involved in all individual rights cases. Steps 4–6 arise only in nonabsolute right opinions.

1. Does the Constitution recognize the claimed right? Is the right a right expressly mentioned in the Constitution or a right implied by the text? What is the scope of the right?
2. Is this right available in the circumstances of this case, and to the kind of people making the claim, e.g., prisoners, schoolchildren?
3. Did the government's policy or practice infringe upon, or impact on the right? Was the impact minimal or more than minimal? (Only the nonabsolute right opinions move on to deal with points 4–6.)
4. What justification does the government offer for adoption of its policy and how important are the interests the government seeks to promote?
5. How important or fundamental is the individual right at stake in the case?
6. What strategy of justification, tests, precedent, and other materials, should be used in crafting the opinion? (See Chapters 3, 4, and 5.)

Problem 1. The very existence of a right is, of course, not disputed when the text of the Constitution itself gives it express recognition. For example, given the text of the First Amendment, no one doubts the existence of a right to freedom of speech. But even in these cases the scope of the right (e.g., does it include the right to sell obscenity?) and whether the right may be invoked by the plaintiff (do prisoners have free speech rights?) remain issues.

But when a claimed right is not even mentioned in the constitutional text, then its very existence, as well as its scope, is in doubt. Take the famous example of a right to use contraception. The word "contraception" does not appear in the Constitution, hence the claim that married and/or single couples have a constitutional right not to be subjected to state criminal penalties for using contraception forces us to engage in constitutional interpretation. One easy solution would be to say that failure of the text to mention the right means there is no such constitutional right. This is a controversial proposition, however, as we shall see in Chapter 4.

A majority of the Supreme Court took an equally controversial but different approach. As one example of how an inferred right can be justified using only "legal" materials, look at Justice Douglas' opinion in *Griswold v. Connecticut* (1965). Justice Douglas began by noting that in previous opinions (precedent) the Court had already engaged in the practice of recognizing the existence of rights not expressly mentioned in the Constitution. He then noted that such rights were inferred in order to make more secure rights expressly mentioned in the Constitution. In other words, he said, the constitutional amendments have "emanations" which form "penumbras" that give the amendments "life and substance." He turned then to the Third, Fourth, Fifth, and Ninth Amendments and found emanating from the specific protections of these amendments (e.g., a right to be free from unreasonable searches, a more general right of privacy). This general right of privacy, he concluded, encorporated the more specific right to use contraception. Well, there you have it: one example of a technique for developing a new right.

Note that the scope of the right of privacy was not fully worked out by the Court in the Connecticut case. Left for determination at a later time were such questions as whether the right to privacy included a right on the part of a woman to terminate her pregnancy with an abortion, or, for example, whether it included the right of a married coupled to engage in oral sex. Arguably, the right of privacy might also include the right of a dying patient to "pull the plug."

Problem 2. Besides recognizing and defining the scope of rights, the Court manages the relationship between government and individual by declaring that a particular right is not available to certain classes of people. Take for example the right to use contraception. In *Griswold* the Court did not address the question whether the right to use contraception would be a right also enjoyed by unmarried sex partners. The decision on this question was left to a later case. (They do have the right.) Similarly, not every free speech right an adult enjoys is available to minors in the context of the public school.

Problem 3. Surprising as it may seem, it is sometimes not clear whether a governmental policy actually infringed a constitutional right. For example, the Court had to decide whether or not the right to use contraception had been infringed by a New York state law that permitted only licensed pharmacists to sell contraception (*Carey v. Population Services International* [1977]). The Court concluded that limiting the distribution of nonprescription contraceptives to licensed pharmacists did impose a severe burden on the right to use contraceptives.

Problem 4. Having concluded that there is a right at stake, that it is a nonabsolute right, and that it was invaded, the Court must now turn to an examination of government's reasons for its actions (i.e., the governmental interests at stake). This step involves the Court in several "suboperations" including the task of discovering what in fact are government's interests at stake. Typically the government's attorney supplies the answer to this question in his or her presentation of the government's case to the Court. For example, in the contraception case Connecticut's attorney said the anti-contraception policy, among other things, served government's interest in prohibiting illicit sexual activities. It is a separate question whether this was the real reason for the anti-contraception law, and whether or not the proferred reason is a sufficient reason to invade the privacy right of married couples. (See Problem 6.)

Problem 5. At some point in the opinion the Court will assess the interests of the individual in the constitutional right at stake. The Court's opinions address this topic by drawing a distinction between ordinary constitutional rights and those rights considered to be "fundamental." If an opinion writer terms a right "fundamental," the opinion writer is less tolerant of the governmental infringement of the right. That is, when an opinion declares the right involved to be fundamental, the opinion writer will only concur in its infringement if the writer concludes that government's policy is backed by interests that are extraordinarily important. On the other hand, the less weighty the right, the less difficult it will be for the opinion writer to find that government's invasion of the right was constitutionally permissible.

In the contraception case the Court concluded that the right of privacy, and the included right of married couples to use contraceptives, was a right of significant importance. This conclusion led the Court to the next step of its opinion, the selection and application of the appropriate test.

Problem 6. The opinion writer now must choose among several justificatory strategies, discussed more fully in Chapter 3. For example, one available alternative is to proceed by balancing the interests of state and individual, and justifying the conclusion by announcing that one set of interests outweighed the other. This was not the approach adopted in the contraception case. In that opinion Justice Douglas declared that, since the right of privacy was fundamental, Connecticut could not pursue the objectives of its policy (reducing illicit sex) by means which swept unnecessarily broadly (i.e., by means which unnecessarily invaded the right to privacy). That is to say, the opinion announced a test or standard of review that the state law had to meet. This test held that laws which infringe fundamental rights will only be upheld if the law pursues its goals by means which are the least restrictive of the rights of the individual.

The opinion then went on to "apply" the test to Connecticut's law. The Court's conclusion was that this law deeply invaded the rights of married couples, and, as the concurring opinions noted, Connecticut had available other less intrusive means to deal with illicit sexual activities. Those other means included simply making adultery and fornication crimes. (These opinions assumed that adultery and fornication could constitutionally be made crimes. This raises a separate problem that must await decision in another case.)

Our brief sketch of how the Court can go and has gone about executing its role of arbitrator of the government–individual relationship is now complete. This sketch leaves out many nuances and complexities, but subsequent chapters will help in filling in the picture of the Court's role in this area.

INTERLUDE: TESTS AND STANDARDS OF REVIEW, A SECOND LOOK

The Supreme Court's individual rights opinions fairly bristle with myriad tests and standards of review. For example, the Court has said that a search without a warrant does not violate an individual's Fourth Amendment protection against unreasonable searches and seizures if the area searched is not one with regard to which (a) the person exhibited an actual expectation of privacy, and (b) that expectation was one that society was prepared to recognize as reasonable. Relying on this test, the Court said that the police may conduct warrantless searches of garbage bags left on the public sidewalk (*California v. Greenwood* [1988]). In another example, the Court has said it will determine whether a punishment violates the prohibition against "cruel and unusual punishments" by taking into account (a) the gravity of the offense and the harshness of the penalty, (b) the sentences imposed on other criminals in the same jurisdiction, and (c) the sentences imposed for commission of the same crime in other jurisdictions (*Solem v. Helm* [1983]).

The Court's free speech opinions rely on different tests depending on the free speech problem involved. I shall take note of only three. The Court has ruled that the right of free speech does not extend to the selling of obscenity. It having become important for the Court to define "obscenity," it developed its famous (infamous?) definition of obscenity. To decide whether a publication is obscene a court must look at "(a) whether 'the average person, applying contemporary community standards' would find the work, taken as a whole, appeals to the prurient interest, (b) whether the work depicts or describes, in a patently offensive way, sexual conduct specifically defined by the applicable state law, and (c) whether the work, taken as a whole, lacks serious literary, artistic, political, or scientific value" (*Miller v. California* [1973]).

Regarding the regulation of "commercial speech" (e.g., an advertisement for a product), the Court has written that commercial speech which concerns an unlawful activity or is misleading is not protected by the First Amendment. But if the speech is about a lawful activity and is not misleading, then state regulation is permissible only if the regulation meets a three-part test: (a) The government interest in regulating the speech must be substantial. (b) The regulation must directly advance the governmental interest. And (c) the regulation must be no more extensive (no tougher) than is necessary to serve the interest (*Central Hudson Gas v. Public Service Comm'n.* [1980]). In subsequent cases the Court interpreted test (c) to mean that government must use means that are narrowly tailored to achieve the desired objective; government is not, however, required to use the least restrictive means (*Board of Trustees of State University of New York v. Fox* [1989]).

Finally, in deciding cases in which, for example, a person has been charged with breach of the peace by giving a speech, the test states that government may only prohibit advocacy when "such advocacy is directed to inciting or producing imminent lawless action and is likely to incite or produce such action" (*Brandenburg v. Ohio* [1969]).

In opinions involving the regulation of business and cases involving the right to "privacy" the Supreme Court uses yet a different set of tests or standards or review. (Lawyers and legal scholars call both these kinds of cases "substantive due process" cases.) These cases involve challenges based on the "due process" clause of the Fourteenth Amendment and involve rights and values not expressly mentioned in the clause but which the Court has seen fit to protect (e.g., privacy and the right to use contraceptives). The two tests the Court relies on in this area are the "rational basis test"—most frequently used in opinions dealing with economic and business regulation—and the "strict scrutiny test"— used in privacy and other lifestyle cases. Both tests would be used in conjunction with Problem 6. I shall discuss each standard of review and then turn to the question of the tests used to select between these standards.

The rational basis test as it operates today imposes on the person challenging government's law, regulation, or policy the burden of persuading the Court of either of two points: (a) that the law or policy does *not* serve a "legitimate" purpose, or (b) that the law or policy is a means which is "not rationally related" to that purpose. (Because the burden of persuading the Court of the unconstitutionality of the law is on the challenger, it is said that the law comes to the Court with a presumption of its being constitutional. In order to win, the challenge must rebut this presumption.) Thus, an opinion justifying *striking down* a law based on this test will conclude either that government's purpose was illegitimate or that the means chosen to seek the purpose was not rationally related to the end, or both. I hasten to add that if the Court uses this standard of review it is in fact very unlikely that the government will lose the case and the challenger win. Almost without fail, when this test is used the law will be found to be constitutionally permissible. In other words, this test is a "lenient" test, and when the Court uses it, the Court *defers* to the legislature's judgment. A Court which behaves in this way is also said to be acting with "restraint."

The Court's opinions dealing with "privacy"—use of contraception, abortions, right to marry—employ a "strict scrutiny" test. When the Court uses this test it says that it is the *government* which must convince the Court both that (a) its policy serves a purpose which is not just legitimate but also compelling, and (b) the means is "necessary" for the achievement of that purpose. Now it is said that the law comes to the Court presumed to be *unconstitutional*. If the law is to survive and not be struck down, government must persuade the Court of the two points in the test.

An opinion relying on the strict scrutiny test and concluding that a law or policy is *un*constitutional will conclude that the purpose of the law was not compelling, that the means chosen was not necessary (other means less harmful to the right involved could have been used), or both. If this is the test used in the opinion, it is unlikely that the Court will uphold the law. This is a "tough" test, hence its name, "strict scrutiny." To use the test suggests that the Court is looking very closely at the law and the justification offered for invading the constitutional right; not many justifications will be accepted as sufficiently strong. A Court using this test is a more "activist" Court.

Let's return to the contraception case. Recall that the *Griswold* opinion concluded there was a right to use contraception (Problem 1), the right was important (Problem 4), and the law infringed the right (Problem 2). The opinion then took up topic 5. Using the "strict scrutiny" test the Court justified striking the law down by saying that the means (barring the use of contraception) chosen by the legislature to pursue its purpose (discouraging adultery and extramarital relations) went too far, "swept too broadly." Thus the Court hinted that there were other "means" for stopping extramarital relations which were less intrusive (e.g., simply making it a crime to engage in adultery).

With these two tests available—the rational basis and strict scrutiny tests—how does the Court explain its choice of one or the other test? I now come to the Court's need to develop a test to choose a test. Roughly speaking, the Court has said it will use the strict scrutiny test when the individual right involved in the dispute is a "fundamental" right, i.e., an especially important right; if the right is a mere ordinary constitutional right, then the Court will use the rational basis test. Thus, some constitutional rights have been designated as fundamental (e.g., the right to privacy, the right to use contraception, the right to an abortion, the right to marry). If the opinion writer classifies the right as fundamental, then the opinion goes on to say that its infringement will be assumed to be unconstitutional and the *government* must persuade the Court not to strike the law down. In other words, the *government* must show that the strict scrutiny test is satisfied. But if the opinion writer does not classify the right as fundamental (e.g., the right to run a business, or the right to engage in homosexual sodomy) then the opinion moves on to use the rational basis test. Now it is the person challenging government's policy who must persuade the Court of the failure of the law to satisfy the rational basis test.

The distinction between which rights and interests are deemed fundamental is one not precisely made in constitutional doctrine. It is frequently said that mere economic rights and interests are not fundamental, but that personal rights are. But the Court has not addressed the question why property is not a fundamental interest (despite its express mention in the Constitution) but privacy is (despite the fact it is not mentioned in the Constitution). Nor has the Court fully explained why it considers the right to interstate travel to be fundamental, while welfare payments are not treated as fundamental.

This discussion hardly exhausts the tests involved in individual rights cases. Other tests appear in the Court's opinions dealing with such topics as free exercise of religion, impairment of contracts, waiver of one's right to have an attorney present when being questioned by the police, right to a hearing before being dismissed from government employment (procedural due process), right not to be subjected to *ex post facto* law-making and bills of attainder.

ENFORCING GOVERNMENT EVEN-HANDEDNESS: EQUAL PROTECTION (FOURTH FEATURE)

Since the beginning of the second half of the twentieth century the Court has played a significant role in policing governmental policies to assure that they do not, without sufficient justification, group people into separate classifications for differential treatment. The Court is given this role most significantly by the Fourteenth Amendment which specifically provides that the *states* shall not deny any person the equal protection of laws. (The Supreme Court interprets the Fifth Amendment's due process clause to impose the same equal protection prohibition on the federal government. And Article IV, Section 2, says that the citizens of each state shall be entitled to all privileges and immunities of citizens in the several states; this provision operates as a kind of equal protection clause to prevent states from arbitrarily denying to nonresidents certain rights and privileges they extend to their own residents.)

The Court's role in enforcing these provisions has not been one of requiring government always to treat everybody the same way. Government could not operate if everybody had to be treated identically.[1] The blind, for example, should not be licensed to drive, and government should be free to provide price supports for farmers but not for automobile companies. Hence the real problem for the Court has been whether government's treating one group of people differently from another has an adequate justification. Put differently, since discrimination is not always unconstitutional, the problem for the Court is to sort out which discriminations may continue and which are unconstitutional.

Again it is possible to characterize the Court's execution of this role as following a series of steps. How these steps relate to each other and build toward a resolution of the case will become clear in a moment.

1. Determination of the criterion used by government to classify people into different groups for differential treatment
2. Determination of the purpose or goal served by government's policy of dividing people into different groups for differential treatment
3. Determining and assessing the effect of the differential treatment on the complaining party
4. Selection of a test or standard of review which is to be used in assessing government's policy
5. Application of that test or standard of review and the statement of a conclusion

Problem 1. Sometimes it is obvious what criterion government has used to classify people for differential treatment. For example, no one would deny that a distinction based on age has been used when the policy expressly states that those over the age of 50 must retire from the police force. Nor is there any doubt that gender is the criterion when the law says that women between the ages of 18–21 may purchase 3.2 beer, but men of the same age may not. But, what if all you

---

[1] The equal protection clause might be interpreted to require that government treat everybody with equal dignity and respect. But fulfilling this requirement does not mean that after full and fair and unprejudiced consideration a policy may not end up granting different benefits to people, or imposing different burdens.

know is that in handing out licenses all 80 of the non-Chinese applicants get the license, but none of the 200 Chinese applicants do? What was the criterion used here? Was it race? Or consider this example. The Bureau of Corrections requires all applicants for the position of prison guard be able to lift 150 lbs. Almost all the women who apply for the position fail the test. Is this a case of discrimination on the basis of gender? What if people who are pregnant are treated differently from those who are not? Is this "gender" discrimination? Or suppose a school board assigns pupils to the school nearest their home. Because blacks and whites live in different sections of the town, this policy has the predictable, the foreseeable, effect of segregating the schools: some schools are virtually all black, others all white. Is this a case of the school board, knowing the foreseeable results of its neighborhood policy, really assigning students on the basis of their race?

When it is not clear what criterion government actually intended to use, the Court must first try to figure this out. To make this determination the justices have resorted to a variety of special tests and rules of thumb. In rough terms, when the Court sees that a policy has had an adverse effect upon, say, the Chinese, women, blacks, it asks (1) whether those adverse effects were foreseeable at the time of the adoption of the policy, and (2) whether government adopted the policy because of, not in spite of, those effects. These are not easy judgments for the Court to make. But at some point in working through the case the Court must decide what exactly it believes was the real criterion used by government for distributing its benefits or burdens.

Problem 2. As the Court moves toward its final determination regarding the constitutionality of the policy, it must also determine the purpose or goal of government's policy. Again, sometimes the answer is easily determined. The government's attorney honestly explains, for example, that imposing the mandatory retirement requirement was designed to help assure that all police are physically up to their demanding jobs. But let's look at the weight-lifting requirement. Assuming the Court has concluded that the weight requirement was in fact a gender criterion, the Court must still examine the question of why government wanted to exclude women from the job of prison guard. Perhaps the answer is easy—male prejudice against women. But perhaps the answer is a set of complex concerns about the effects the presence of women would have in an all-male penal institution. In any event, the Court will determine, for good or ill, the goal(s) of government's policy.

Problem 3. Assessing the impact of differential treatment upon the complaining party is also sometimes easy (e.g., the complainant loses or fails to get a job). But sometimes the effects are more complex, subtle, and arguably even more far-reaching. Take the example of racial segregation in the public schools. Excluding black students from attending school with white students certainly has the effect of limiting the range of schools both black and white can consider attending. But, in addition, this forced separation of the races may very well have deep and damaging (albeit, different) psychological effects on black and white pupils (*Brown v. Board of Education* [1954]).

Problem 4. Having determined the criterion used by government, government's purpose, and the effects of government's policy, the Court now moves on to a different phase. It starts the business of evaluating or assessing government's policy. To do this it adopts as its measuring rod, its scale, a test or standard of review.

Speaking roughly and in perhaps too general terms, the Court tends to use a different test or standard of review in connection with different kinds of equal protection cases. That is to say, the Court's opinions can be classified into three groups:

Group I
- Cases in which a racial criterion is used to the disadvantage of a racial minority
- Cases in which a racial criterion is used as part of an affirmative action plan
- Cases in which the difference in treatment affects a fundamental right/ interest and may also have an impact on the poor
- Cases in which the criterion is phrased in terms of illegitimacy or citizenship[2]

Group II
- Cases in which a gender criterion is used to the disadvantage of women or men
- Cases in which a gender criterion is used as part of an affirmative effort to help women

Group III
- All other cases, such as those involving the regulation of business, or the use of age as a criterion

In rough terms, the opinions in Group I use an equal protection version of the strict scrutiny test.

As with the other strict scrutiny test the burden of persuasion is on the government. For the law to be upheld government must convince the Court that

---

[2]One might wonder why cases that involve differences of treatment based on gender or handicap are not included in this group of cases. This is an important question that has been the subject of dispute among the justices.

(i) its policy serves a "compelling" purpose, and (ii) that the criterion used, the classification scheme, and the differences in treatment are "necessary" to serve that purpose.

When this test is used, the government's policy is presumed unconstitutional unless the government can satisfy its burden of persuasion.

The opinions in Group II use what is called the middle level test.

The government must persuade the Court that (i) its policy serves an "important" purpose, and (ii) that the criterion used and the difference in treatment is "substantially related" to the purpose.

When this test is used, the government's policy is presumed unconstitutional unless the government can satisfy its burden of persuasion, which is now lighter than under the previous test.

The Group III opinions use the equal protection version of a rational basis test.

The person challenging the law must convince the Court that either that (i) the purpose of the law is not legitimate, or, that (ii) the criterion and classification scheme is not "rationally related" to the purpose.

The use of this test means government's policy is presumed to be constitutional unless the complaining party can convince the Court otherwise.

Problem 5. The last step is the application of the test or standard of review to determine whether government's policy is constitutional. This is no mechanical step, since determining whether a policy's purpose is, for example, compelling is a difficult problem in judgment. And, in fact, the Court has said little about how it goes about deciding when a government's policy is either compelling, or important, or merely legitimate. Similarly, there is no simple way to determine whether the classification established by government's policy was "necessary," or substantially related to its purpose, or merely "rationally related" to its purpose. But this is the language that the Court has chosen to use in justifying its equal protection decisions. It is a language that may, in fact, cover up or fail to reveal adequately what in fact the justices were thinking about when they reached their decision.

SUPERVISING GOVERNMENT'S RELATIONSHIP WITH RELIGION (FIFTH FEATURE)

The First Amendment specifies that "Congress shall make no law respecting an establishment of religion, or prohibiting the free exercise thereof. . . ." Interpreting these clauses and deciding on government's proper relationship to religion is one of the more sensitive political problems the Court has faced over the years. And it is a task that has brought the Court considerable criticism as it has had to respond to persistent governmental efforts to support religious activities as well as governmental policies that have limited the free exercise of religion. There is no easy and nondistorting way to describe the relationship the Court has shaped between government and religion, but perhaps a metaphor will help capture the complexities. Rather than having established a ''wall of separation'' between government and religion (a phrase used by Thomas Jefferson), the Court has erected a fence with many gates in it. Those gates, on the one hand, permit government to reach out to a limited extent to support religious activities, and, on the other hand, permit religious concerns to cross to the other side to influence and limit government. Thus, for example, government today may lend textbooks to students attending private religious schools, and may exempt church property from taxation; at the same time, religious concerns may, to an extent, enter into the formulation of public policy.

The Court erected this rather permeable barrier through the use of yet another set of tests or standards of review. The derivation of the tests used in conjunction with the ''establishment clause'' opinions has been the subject of much controversy both on and off the Court. The text, framers' intent, the theory and principles of the First Amendment, tradition, contemporary values, precedent, and practical considerations have all figured into the debate over the development, interpretation, and application of the tests. It is these debates which characterize many of the recent majority and dissenting opinions.

The tests in dispute in connection with the establishment clause are the so-called Lemon tests (based on the name of an opinion in which they appeared, *Lemon v. Kurtzman* [1971]). To survive a challenge based on the establishment clause, the policy must (1) have a secular purpose; (2) its primary effect must be one that neither advances nor inhibits religion; and (3) the law must not foster excessive governmental entanglement with religion.

Just as the derivation of these tests has been the subject of much dispute, so has their interpretation and application. For example, the justices have argued over the application of the first test and the question of what are acceptable methods of proving that government was motivated by a desire to promote religion. (Any test which calls for proof of an improper motive raises similar problems of proof, e.g., proving an intent to discriminate on the basis of race.) And shifting majorities on the Court has meant widely divergent and conflicting results which leave the Court open to considerable criticism. For example, the Court has issued opinions justifying the loan of textbooks to religious private schools, but not the loan of maps; one opinion permits government support for the transportation of students to private religious schools, but another prohibits financing transportation to take those same children on field trips; public schools may not begin the school day with a prayer, but a state legislature may; and schools may not post the Ten Commandments on their walls, but the city may pay for a Christmas display in a park that includes a nativity scene.

Turning to the free exercise clause, these cases generally involve a state law or policy that does not discriminate on the basis of religion but has an especially acute impact on a religious person or group. The affected person or group now asks that they be exempted from the law's coverage. For example, the state's policy may say that no one may collect unemployment compensation who voluntarily leaves a job. Now, the question arises whether this policy may be constitutionally applied to a person who leaves a job in a munitions factory because of religious objections to war. Must this person, in the name of the free exercise of religion, be excused from the state's policy and be allowed to collect unemployment compensation. (Yes.)

The modern Court's use of tests in justifying its decisions in such cases goes as follows (*Thomas v. Review Board of Indiana Employment Security* [1980]). The burden is first placed on the religious objector to establish that (a) his or her claim for an exemption is based on a religious belief and not on a mere philosophical or other nonreligious belief; (b) the religious claim is sincerely held; and (c) the objector must show that continued enforcement of the policy does and will have a real impact on his or her free exercise of religion. The Court says that only if it is convinced of these points will it now listen to what the state must establish. Assuming the religious objectors have been convincing, the burden of persuasion switches to the state which must now, in order to avoid an exemption being granted, meet the terms of a strict scrutiny test. That is to say, the state must now prove that the uniform enforcement of the policy without exception is "necessary" for the realization of a "compelling" state purpose.

GETTING THE SUPREME COURT
TO PLAY ITS ROLE

The Supreme Court has played five essential roles. Now it is time to look at the mechanics and procedures by which the Court is brought into the policy-making process.

The Supreme Court in sharp contrast to the other branches of the federal government may not on its own initiative thrust itself into a policy arena and start issuing opinions announcing that this policy is constitutionally permissible but that policy is not. The Court may only act when a suit is initiated by someone else and brought to the Court for resolution. To see how these cases get into the Supreme Court we need to take a quick look at the federal judicial system.

A Snapshot of the Federal Judicial System

The federal judicial system consists of four basic types of court—a small number of specialized federal courts which deal with such specific matters as customs and patent appeals; 95 federal district courts found in all 50 states; 13 U.S. courts of appeal; and the United States Supreme Court. Our discussion will omit any further description of the specialized courts.

The federal district courts are the trial courts of the federal system (i.e., the courts where legal action originates, where evidence is received, witnesses questioned, and the first legal judgment in the case reached). There are today 95 federal district courts (staffed by almost 600 judges)—90 in the states, one in the District of Columbia, and four in the U.S. Territories (Guam, the Virgin Islands, the Northern Marianas, and Puerto Rico). States with more than one federal district court are divided into separate parts so that one court might be the U.S. District Court for Western New York and another the federal district court for the southern district. These courts have both criminal and civil jurisdiction. Thus, though these courts try a variety of different kinds of cases, for our purposes we need only note that the federal district courts will try civil suits involving a "federal question," a federal constitutional issue, or one arising under a federal statute, as well as federal criminal cases. Federal courts do not take cases raising exclusively an issue of state law. Pure state law cases must originate in a state court and will not be reviewed by the U.S. Supreme Court.

A constitutional law case touching on a matter of civil (i.e., noncriminal) law, typically, is begun in the federal district courts when a complaint is filed alleging that some law, policy, or action of a branch of the federal, state, or local government is unconstitutional. Constitutional issues arise in different ways in the criminal context. In these cases the whole conflict may get under way when the federal or state government charges and prosecutes someone for a crime. At this point the criminally accused may raise a constitutional challenge to the criminal law he or she is accused of having violated. More commonly the accused claims that the police acted illegally, violating that person's rights under the Fourth or Fifth Amendments, as when, for example, the accused says he was improperly questioned without a lawyer present, or evidence was illegally seized. A constitutional issue also arises when the accused says that the trial itself was conducted in violation of a constitutional provision (i.e., he was not provided an attorney at state expense).

However the constitutional issue is first raised, it is the resolution of that issue by the trial court which may then be appealed to the second tier of the federal system with general jurisdiction, the U.S. courts of appeal. The 13 U.S. courts of appeal are the intermediate appellate courts between the federal district courts and the highest appellate court, the Supreme Court. Congress has divided the country geographically into twelve circuits, including the District of Columbia, with each state assigned to a circuit. (The 13th circuit, the Federal Circuit, consists of three specialized federal courts.) There are approximately 160 appeals court judges assigned in varying numbers to the different circuits. Appeals are normally heard by groups of three judges, but cases are heard *en banc*, meaning all the judges assigned to the circuit hear the case (up to a limit of, say, nine judges).

Generally speaking, the losing party in a federal district court has the right to appeal to the appropriate U.S. court of appeals. That is, the appeal must be to the court of appeals with jurisdiction over the particular federal district court which had original jurisdiction. Thus a decision by the Southern District of New York must be appealed to the Second Circuit. These appeals courts also hear appeals from decisions from federal administrative agencies, such as the Federal Communications Commission. One may not appeal simply because one is unhappy with the result; the appeal must raise a claim of a legal error committed by the lower tribunal. As appellate courts these courts do not re-try the case, do not collect new evidence, do not reexamine the witnesses; they only review the printed transcript of the proceedings in the federal district court and look at the evidence already presented in that proceeding to determine whether the federal district court made any errors of law (e.g., misinterpreted precedent, a statute, or the Constitution itself).

Before we turn to the Supreme Court you should be aware of the fact that states have their own multi-tiered judicial systems, systems that comprise specialized courts, trial courts, and several levels of appellate courts, including usually a single highest state court. (Texas is an exception with two highest courts, one for civil and one for criminal cases.) Issues of federal law and the constitutionality of federal and state laws under the U.S. Constitution may be raised in the state courts. (One may not challenge a federal law on the grounds it violates the *state* constitution, since federal law is supreme pursuant to the U.S. Constitution.) The Supreme Court may review state court decisions dealing with the constitutionality of federal and state laws under the U.S. Constitution.

The Jurisdiction of the Supreme Court

The Supreme Court's jurisdiction is of two sorts. Article III, Section 2 of the Constitution gives the Court *original jurisdiction* in certain cases. (Original jurisdiction extends to cases affecting ambassadors, ministers, consuls, and cases in which a state is a party.) Only some two hundred cases have arisen in the Court's original jurisdiction. Nothing more will be said here about original jurisdiction.

Constitutional law deals primarily with cases arising under the Court's *appellate jurisdiction* (i.e., those cases in which the Supreme Court is asked to review the decisions of other courts for errors of law). Article III, Section 2 grants the Court appellate jurisdiction subject to "such Exceptions, and under such Regulations, as Congress shall make." Pursuant to its appellate jurisdiction the Supreme Court reviews constitutional issues raised in both the federal and state court systems.

To get the Court to review a case a petitioner must file a writ of certiorari, which is merely a request made to the Court that it exercise its discretion to hear the case. A writ of certiorari can be filed to seek review of the following types of decisions (28 U.S.C. §§ 1254, 1257):

- All cases decided by *federal* courts of appeals
- A case decided by the highest *state* court where the validity of a treaty or statute of the United States is drawn in question on grounds of it being repugnant to the Constitution, treaties, or law of the United States

Review on this basis is not a matter of right, and will only be granted if four justices agree that the controversy is of sufficient importance for the Court to review the case.[3] The Court denies most petitions for certiorari. Denial of a writ of certiorari is not a decision "on the merits" (i.e., does not necessarily mean the Court approves of the correctness of the decision in the case being appealed). Technical considerations having nothing to do with the merits of the case may be the basis of the denial (*Maryland v. Baltimore Radio Show* [1950]).

(Incidentally, until 1988 there were two routes into the Supreme Court. One set of cases followed the "appeal" basis for review, and for these cases review was mandatory by the Supreme Court. When a case came to the Supreme Court under its "mandatory appellate" jurisdiction, the party appealing was called the *appellant*, and the other party, the *appellee*. All other cases had to follow the certiorari route. If a case came to the Court via a writ of certiorari, then the party seeking reversal was the *petitioner*, and the other was the *respondent*. In 1988 Congress eliminated the mandatory appellate jurisdiction of the Supreme Court in order to let the Court decide for itself just which cases it would and would not hear.)

Having been accepted for review, the case proceeds as follows: Appellant/petitioner and appellee/respondent file briefs (written legal arguments which must follow a prescribed format), and the two sides then present their positions orally before the entire nine-member Supreme Court (each side is usually allotted only one-half hour to speak). The case is now ready for decision by the Supreme Court.

The Supreme Court's Processes of Decision Making and Justification

In a book entitled *The Judicial Decision* (1961) Richard Wasserstrom draws a distinction between the "the process of discovery" and "the process of justification."[4] Processes of *discovery* are those processes involved in hitting upon the

---

[3] In addition to the requirements just noted, the Court will not review a case, and will not permit the lower federal courts to take a case, that does not meet other requirements. The suit must involve a real dispute between genuinely adverse parties one of which has been injured, or faces an immediate threat of injury to a legal right. This statement roughly summarizes a body of constitutional law touching on the question of whether a litigant has "standing" to invoke the authority of a federal court. Note, besides this "standing" requirement the case must meet certain other requirements. It must not be "moot"; it must be "ripe"; it must involve a genuine "case" or "controversy," must not involve a "political question," and must satisfy other jurisdictional requirements.

[4] Richard A. Wasserstrom, *The Judicial Decision* (Stanford, Cal.: Stanford University Press, 1961).

judgment, the bottom line, e.g., the petitioner should win. Processes of *justification* are processes used for publicly giving reasons in support of the judgment. In a cynical view of the relationship of the two processes, the process of justification merely involves a rationalization of a decision that may have been reached for entirely different and undisclosed reasons. The reasons publicly given for the decision need not have, and probably did not affect, determine, or cause the decision reached. An alternative view holds that a judge begins with a vaguely formed conclusion, tries to find premises and arguments to support it, and, if the judge cannot find sound arguments, the judge may reject the conclusion and seek another. If one accepts this view, then the reasons for the decision may have a bearing on the judgment. Thus, there are important reasons for being concerned about the kinds of justifications used and the criteria of an adequate justification. Not the least of these reasons is the fact that these opinions are binding precedent for the lower federal courts and state courts.

After reading the briefs and hearing the oral argument, the Supreme Court justices discuss and vote on the case at a conference. What leads an individual justice to vote a certain way on a particular case is part of the process of discovery. Once the vote is taken the justices have entered into the process of justification. Who has the responsibility of writing this public justification, the opinion? If the Chief Justice votes with the majority (five or more of the nine justices) it is his or her prerogative to assign the task of drafting the majority opinion. The Chief Justice may assign the task to himself or to another justice in the majority. If the Chief Justice votes with the minority, then the most senior justice in the majority has this prerogative.

In fact, this voting process and the switching of votes that can take place after the conference may produce a number of different kinds of voting patterns and, accordingly, opinions. The vote may be unanimous and result in a single opinion signed by all nine members. The Court might also be split into a majority (five or more members) and a minority. When this occurs several different types of opinion may be written:

- There may be a single majority opinion (signed by all the justices in the majority) and a single dissenting opinion (signed by all the dissenters). There may also be several dissenting opinions disagreeing with the majority judgment for different reasons.
- A split Court might also result in a somewhat different set of opinions: There may be a single majority opinion, dissenting opinions, and, in addition, one or more special concurrences. In this situation the writer of the special concurrence agrees with the majority on the judgment and the majority's reasoning, but writes separately to add his or her own thoughts for special emphasis on a point important to the writer.
- The majority might also be made up of five justices who agree on the judgment and the reasons therefore, plus other justices who agree with the

judgment only. They may write a separate concurring opinion which offers a different set of reasons for the same judgment. Concurring opinions do not have the force of law.

Occasionally the Court is so badly split there is no majority opinion. In these situations there may only be a majority which agrees in the judgment alone (e.g., petitioner wins, but there is no majority in support of a set of reasons for this outcome). In this case, the justices who comprise the majority supporting the judgment only may split themselves up in such a way that there is a *plurality* opinion signed by, say, three justices, and one or more concurring opinions agreeing in the judgment, but for different reasons. There, of course, may still be in this situation one or more dissenting opinions. Without a majority agreeing upon a set of reasons for the judgment, the results in this case have less value as a precedent. Deciding what constitutes authoritatively established doctrine in this situation requires careful interpretation of the plurality and other concurring opinions.

How complex matters can become is illustrated by *Regents of University of California v. Bakke* (1978). Justice Powell wrote "the Court's" opinion, but he was the only justice who fully agreed with everything in that opinion. Roughly speaking, one group of four other justices agreed with part of what he had to say (but for different reasons), making a majority of five on part of what the opinion announced. These same justices disagreed with other parts of the opinion. But a different set of justices agreed with another part of the judgment reached by Powell, but, again, for different reasons. Thus another block of five, including Powell, supported part of what Justice Powell wrote and dissented as to part. As this case shows, justices can write opinions which concur in the judgment in part and yet also dissent.

Mention should also be made of the per curiam ("for the Court") opinion which announces the judgment of the majority in a brief unsigned opinion. This opinion may be accompanied by nine separate concurring and dissenting opinions for a total of ten, the maximum number of opinions possible in a single case. (*New York Times Co. v. United States* [1971]).

The processes of opinion drafting are, as one might expect, both complex and fluid. The justice assigned to write the majority opinion drafts an opinion (with the assistance of one or more law clerks) which he or she then circulates for review and comment by the other justices in the majority. The dissenters also begin drafting their opinion(s). These initial drafts may go through many revisions, and, in the course of the process the justices may switch their votes. Coalitions may form, disintegrate, and new coalitions form. What had started out as the majority opinion may have to be converted to a dissenting opinion. A justice may begin justifying the decision one way only to end up writing a different justification. Severe and angry conflict may arise as the justices in the majority seek to forge a single umbrella under which they can all live comfortably. Justice Holmes said of the process that "the boys generally cut one of the genitals" out of his opinions.[5] However difficult the process of opinion writing, evidence of the justices' struggle usually does not appear in the opinion. In fact, the late Justice Black advised Justice Blackmun as follows: "Harry, never display agony in public in an opinion. Always write it as though it's clear as crystal."[6]

Thus, interpretation of the Constitution is a political act in several respects. First, it involves internal bargaining over the shape of the opinions to be issued. Second, to interpret the Constitution and act on that interpretation has direct consequences in the world on real people, real institutions, affects who gets what, when, and how. Life and death, wealth and fortune, war and peace, dignity and respect, and freedom and liberty are among the matters at stake in constitutional disputes. The justices understand and perceive that the significance of their decisions extends beyond the parties before them to additional untold millions of people; it can effect the institutions of government, the Court itself, and the nation as a whole.

Furthermore, the act of interpretation itself is one which unavoidably entails the applying of theories of law, language and interpretation, justice, morality, and politics to specific problems and choices. Beyond this, the act of interpretation involves calling upon a general understanding of the world, human beings, the workings and sociology of the society, historical perspectives, and tradition. Take one example. To decide whether the Constitution's proscriptions against "cruel and inhuman punishment" should be read to prohibit capital punishment requires a justice to develop (albeit sometimes subconsciously) a theory of constitutional interpretation which itself entails a philosophy of law and language. The justice must also develop an understanding of theories of punishment and insight into the actual effects and sociological consequences of capital punishment as carried out by the modern-day criminal justice system against a background of social, economic, and racial inequalities.

BASIC FEATURES OF A SUPREME
COURT OPINION

This chapter concludes with a review of the standard elements common to the Court's opinions. First is the *title*. The name of the opinion is based on the names of the parties to the controversy. The party listed first is the one who seeks reversal of the lower court decision, whereas the second-named party seeks to have that decision affirmed. Recall that the parties seeking reversal and affirmance may be called appellant and appellee, or petitioner and respondent, respectively.

---

[5] Quoted in Walter F. Murphy, James E. Fleming, Esq., and William F. Harris, II, *American Constitutional Interpretation* (Mineola, N.Y.: The Foundation Press, 1986), p. 60.
[6] Quoted in Howard Ball, *Courts and Politics* (Englewood Cliffs, N.J.: Prentice-Hall, 1987), p. 277.

A useful tip: At this point look for an indication in the opinion as to whether the lower court's decision was affirmed or reversed; whether the appellant/petitioner won, or whether the appellee/respondent won. Knowing this helps make more sense of the opinion.

The next major element is the recitation of *the facts of the case*: who did what to whom, when, how, and why. The opinion will also make mention of any relevant statutes, regulations, or policies involved in the dispute. Note that the justices may disagree in their characterization and interpretation of the facts of the case. Thus one may find that the majority opinion describes the facts of the case differently from the dissenting opinions, and perhaps even differently from the concurring opinions. A complete view of what is involved in the case may only be possible by piecing together the factual statements of all these opinions. Note that sometimes these facts are not all discussed in one place in any given opinion; the justices may add important facts to be considered at any point in their opinion.

Be sure to get a fix on the *procedural history* of the case. The opinion will describe who complained and what the result was in the trial court, who appealed to an intermediate appeals court and what the result was there. And the opinion will make clear who is now appealing or petitioning to the Supreme Court. Understanding this sequence of events will help in understanding the remaining parts of the opinion. Especially important is who seeks review in the Supreme Court.

Next, look for the *legal claims* made in the case. What did the plaintiff claim and the defendant respond? What are the claims on appeal of *the appellant/petitioner and the response of the appellee/respondent*? An opinion will briefly summarize the constitutional challenge being raised in the case. Look for the specific section of the Constitution said to have been violated and why the appellant/petitioner thinks it has been violated. Also be aware of the response of the appellee/respondent. Be careful to note that the appellant/petitioner may have raised several different constitutional claims involving different parts of the Constitution. As to a given claim, note that the appellant/petitioner may have made different, alternative arguments supporting the same claim. These different parts of the appellant/petitioner's case may be discussed at different points in an opinion.

You are now in a position to look for the *issues* in the case. The issues are those questions which the party seeking reversal would answer differently from the party seeking to affirm the decision. Answer the question(s) one way, and the appellant/petitioner wins; answer another way, the appellee/respondent wins. But, be careful. Sometimes the opinion itself expressly states the issues ("The issue in this case is. . . ."); sometimes not. You may have to figure out the issues yourself. And sometimes you might conclude, upon reflection, that the opinion's phrasing of an issue is too vague, inaccurate, or misleading. Sometimes the majority, concurring, and/or dissenting justices disagree over the phrasing of the crucial issue. For example, one justice may say the crucial issue in the case is whether the *plaintiff* has shown that government's differential treatment of men and women, in requiring draft registration of men but not women, does not serve an important purpose. Another justice might say the issue is whether the *defendant* government has shown that including women from the registration program would impede its purposes in having a draft registration program (*Rostker v. Goldberg* [1981]).

We come now to the main body of the opinion. These sections of the opinion announce the Court's decision, and outline the remedy (if any). In these sections the Court justifies the decision and remedy by providing its answers to the issues. The Court may comment upon, analyze, and react to the arguments of the parties to the case. The opinion may accept, reject, modify, or ignore these arguments. As part of this justificatory effort you will find the Court using rules, principles, doctrines, tests, and standards of review. (These concepts will be discussed further in Chapter 5.) It is these sections of the opinion that establish the precedent value of the case and provide the interpretation of the Constitution that will be used in the future in connection with additional cases. The remaining chapters of this book are a further exploration of this aspect of a Supreme Court opinion.

Law students are frequently encouraged, if not required, to "brief" the cases they are assigned to read. A brief is nothing but a short summary of a judicial opinion, a way to take notes on a case. These briefs can be organized in different ways, but one form a brief can take is as follows:

- Name of case and date
- Facts of the case (who did what to whom, when, why, how, etc. Included in the description of the facts should be mention of the specific law, policy, or action being challenged as unconstitutional and the claims as to why the law, policy or action is unconstitutional.)
- The vote (number of justices in the majority, number concurring, dissenting; author of the majority opinion, and authors of the other opinions)
- Procedural history of the case (decision in federal district court, decision in court of appeals, who is appealing to the Supreme Court)
- Issues or questions
- The answers to the questions given by the majority
- Summary of the majority opinion's reasoning
- Summaries of significant other opinions (concurring, dissenting)

Briefing serves an important purpose besides providing one with a handy synopsis of an opinion. The very effort put into briefing a case helps to focus the mind on what is truly important in the opinion. Briefing is, thus, a useful form of self-discipline for the inexperienced legal researcher. The more experienced researcher recognizes that briefing holds important traps for the unwary. This is so because the attempt to reduce a complex opinion from 30 pages to one or two unavoidably means that much important material never finds it way into the brief. Briefs can serve as handy reminders of the content of an opinion, but they cannot substitute for a more extended description and analysis.

CONSTITUTIONALITY OF FEDERAL AND STATE LAW: AN ADDENDUM

A governmental policy, in order to be constitutional, must have been enacted in conformity with the requirements of the Constitution. What follows is one way to summarize those basic requirements.

Thus for a *federal* law or policy to be constitutionally permissible under the federal Constitution it must

1. be enacted according to the proper steps and procedures. If, for example, a particular law was enacted by Congress, the passage of the law must have conformed to the processes established in the Constitution for the enactment of legislation; and
2. be authorized either by
   a. explicit powers delegated by the text of the Constitution, or
   b. the powers reasonably implied by the text of the Constitution, or
   c. the residuum of inherent power on which government may call to preserve the polity; and
3. violate neither
   a. any of the specific prohibitions of the Constitution text, nor
   b. any of the rights properly implied in the Constitution.[7]

In addition, those who take a broad view of the Constitution would be inclined to add an additional requirement at this point:

   c. nor violate those "natural rights" that people have irrespective of the form of government that surrounds them and are arguably incorporated into the Constitution itself and are just as binding as the document's plain words.

The criteria for finding a *state* law, policy, or practice constitutional under the federal Constitution are different. A state policy, law, or practice in order to be constitutionally permissible under the federal Constitution must

---

[7] Adapted from Walter F. Murphy, James E. Fleming, Esq., and William F. Harris, II, *American Constitutional Interpretation* (Mineola, N.Y.: The Foundation Press, 1986), pp. 31–32.

1. not be preempted or be superseded by any federal statute or other federal action with the force of law, nor
2. exceed limits on state authority by invading the powers granted to the national government, nor
3. violate either
   a. any of the specific prohibitions of the constitutional document, or
   b. any of the rights properly implied in the Constitution.

And, as noted above, those who take a broad view of the Constitution would add an additional requirement at this point:

   c. nor violate those "natural rights" that people have irrespective of the form of government that surrounds them and are arguably incorporated into the Constitution.

For a law, policy, or action to be constitutional it must meet all the relevant criteria. Failure of, for example, a federal or state statute to meet any of the relevant criteria means that this statute is unconstitutional.

CHAPTER 2

Opinion Writing
in the Supreme Court

This chapter continues the discussion of judicial opinion writing by looking at the practice from the perspective of a justice of the Supreme Court. The assumption is that if one can understand the problems of writing a Supreme Court opinion from the perspective of a justice, one is placed in an improved position as a *reader* to understand and appreciate other opinions.

WRITING A SUPREME COURT OPINION:
THE GENERAL PROBLEM

Courts, including the Supreme Court, could operate by simply declaring a winner in the dispute before them—"petitioner wins"—without offering any explanation or justification for the decision. But for the Supreme Court to operate this way would leave the lower and future Supreme Courts with no guidance. In the absence of an opinion we are left to guess the principles of law at work; we have little by which to guide our future behavior; we remain uncertain regarding what the Court will do in new cases involving similar but not identical disputes. When the decision is of great political significance, but unaccompanied by a persuasive opinion, the Court's decision may continue to rankle significant portions of the population making more difficult acceptance of the result. Written constitutional opinions can and do have an important educational and moral function which would obviously be lost if the Court merely declared winners and losers without explanation. Constitutional litigation is not a boxing match in which the judges announce the victor leaving the loser to declare without insight into the decision that "I was robbed."

These comments help set the stage for the problem facing the justices. The justices are expected to write opinions which explain the dispute before them and which are persuasive justifications of the decision reached. All this must be accomplished within certain constraints and expectations which sharply limit the ways in which a justice may go about offering such a justification. It is these constraints and expectations which importantly work to make a judicial opinion different from the kinds of explanation and justification one might offer when settling a dispute among children, or a philosopher might offer in reaching a conclusion on a moral issue. In the absence of these constraints and expectations the justices' opinions could look like any other justification—moral, theological, political, economic, or practical. In other words, it is these constraints and expectations which lead a justice to write a *legal* opinion. This is not to say that a legal opinion is amoral, or apolitical, or otherwise impractical. It is to say that the constraints and expectations bearing down on the justices lead them to use a special legal language, certain kinds of materials, and certain modes of reasoning and analysis. The justices consequently produce opinions written in a style, fashion, and custom which reflect a long tradition of judicial craftsmanship.

Let's examine this tradition by beginning with some general requirements an opinion writer has to satisfy. The opinion would have to have a name, for example, *Brandenburg v. Ohio* (1969), with the name of the petitioner listed first. A justice is then expected to provide a description of the facts of the case (who did what to whom, when, how, why, etc.) including mention of the relevant statutes, regulations, policies, decisions, or actions that were involved in the dispute and might be the subject of the constitutional challenge. Readers of an opinion also want to know what it was the complaint stated—what exactly it was that the complaining party said had been done which was unconstitutional, which constitutional provision(s) allegedly had been violated and, what argument was offered to support the claim of unconstitutionality. Now the readers will want to know what it is the government said in response—what it said by way of fending off the constitutional challenge. At this point in the opinion the justice would be in a position to identify the issues at stake—the questions raised by the competing arguments. It is these questions to which the competing parties suggest different answers and to which the opinion writer will have to provide a judicial answer in the rest of the opinion. Next, the readers will want to know what the trial court and the intermediate court of appeals decided.

I will now illustrate what has been said to this point. Brandenburg had been arrested for giving a speech advocating white racism and suggesting the need for violence to protect the interests of the white race. He delivered his speech at a KKK rally at which some of the members of the audience carried weapons. Brandenburg was charged with violating Ohio's Criminal Syndicalism statute "for advocating the duty, necessity, or propriety of crime, sabotage, violence, or unlawful methods of terrorism as a means of accomplishing industrial or political reform." At his trial on the "criminal syndicalism" charge, Brandenburg claimed that the arrest and enforcement of this statute was a violation of his First Amendment right to engage in freedom of speech; thus he asked that the charge be dismissed. Brandenburg was in fact fined $100 and sentenced to one to ten years' imprisonment. The Supreme Court of Ohio dismissed Brandenburg's appeal on the grounds that there was no substantial constitutional question in the case. Brandenburg sought review in the Supreme Court.

Brandenburg argued that prior Supreme Court cases relevant to this sort of problem established the principle that government may only criminally punish a person for delivering a speech advocating the use of force when there is a clear and present danger of lawless action. Brandenburg argued that his speech was not likely to produce such action. The prosecutor, however, saw in Brandenburg's speech a clear threat of lawless action.

The central issues in the case on appeal to the Supreme Court, thus, were (1) the appropriate test for determining the constitutionality of the state's conviction and (2) the application of that test to this case (i.e., whether or not the speech Brandenburg gave created a clear and present danger of lawless action).

The materials in the previous paragraph appear in the Supreme Court's opinion before it turns to the central issue and offers a justification for the reversal of the appellate court decision. It is at this point in the opinion that the real demands of judicial craftsmanship arise. Let's turn to these expectations and constraints before returning to the drafting of the opinion in *Brandenburg*.

CONSTRAINTS AND EXPECTATIONS

It should go without saying that the decision should be the "correct" decision; as a substantive matter the opinion should be one that gains critical and popular assent. But this essential point aside—the point being addressed here is that the style or the manner of writing-up and justifying a legally correct resolution of the dispute should satisfy certain constraints and expectations.

- If the opinion is to be the majority opinion and authoritatively establish constitutional doctrine, it must gain the assent of at least five of the nine participating justices.

  Note: the guidelines which follow apply to majority, plurality, concurring, and dissenting opinions.
- The opinion should be directed to resolving only the dispute and the issues before the Court. The opinion should not examine a wide range of unrelated First Amendment free speech issues. But the opinion should cover the necessary topics for resolving a dispute of this sort. (See, for example, Chapter 1, pp. 14, 20.)
- The justices should craft the opinion in a way to provide guidance for future federal and state court judges, as well as lawyers and the populace at large.

- The decision should have the appearance of being determined by considerations external to a justice's personal desires and will. The arguments the justices offer should be arguments based on law, doctrines, principles, values, which are not just a matter of personal preference and desire. It is the law that justices are expected to pronounce, not their colleagues' personal preferences in this dispute.
- The opinion should make use of, or take account of, those "materials" the legal community (and society) accepts as the appropriate materials for writing opinions and developing legal arguments. For example, the opinion should take account of relevant precedent.
- The opinion should not use other "materials" the legal community (and society) considers inappropriate bases upon which to build a legal argument. For example, an opinion that was based on the Bible or the Koran would be viewed as not having used appropriate legal materials.
- The justices should write the opinion so that it is persuasive. It must offer a set of reasons and logically constructed arguments for the result reached.
- A justice will want to draft an opinion that is not obviously inconsistent with views he or she personally expressed in previous opinions, nor obviously inconsistent with precedent in general, unless the opinion specifically overrules precedent. Furthermore, the views the justices express in this opinion should be ones with which they can live in the future.

Crafting the Opinion

Because a majority opinion must attract the vote of at least five members of the Court, the drafter of the opinion faces a difficult challenge. If there is not substantial agreement among the justices on how the decision is to be justified, then there may be no majority opinion, but only, perhaps, a plurality opinion and one or more concurring opinions. But let's assume that the justices are not so deeply divided over how the result in the case should be justified. Nevertheless, it is frequently the case that justices disagree among themselves over how precisely the justification should be phrased. Consequently the justices will inevitably have to compromise, to engage in some bargaining over the crafting of the opinion. (Recall at this point Chapter 1's description of the opinion writing process.) Each word, phrase, sentence, and paragraph could be the subject of careful consideration and deliberate, conscious choice and agreement. As a consequence, some things may be deliberately phrased in general or ambiguous terms to insure agreement among the five justices. Furthermore, arguments one justice might have wanted to include in the opinion may have to be dropped. Yet other points and arguments a justice personally did not want to use might have to be included.

This bargaining process can produce opinions which upon careful analysis can be shown to be internally contradictory, or at least not fully explicable. This is an important point: one cannot automatically assume that each Supreme Court opinion is wholly coherent, totally free from internal contradictions, or free from inexplicable statements that can only be accounted for by understanding the bargaining that must have taken place.

The opinion might also take the form of an umbrella under which the justices in the majority can comfortably fit. Thus the final majority opinion might include not one central argument justifying the result, but several different arguments—arguments not inconsistent with each other, but not fully integrated either. Sometimes this umbrella is constructed by "arguing in the alternative." That is, the opinion may mount one argument in support of the result, only then move on to say something like the following: "*Even if* we do not rely on our previous argument, we conclude that the decision below should be reversed (or affirmed) for the following reasons." (For the reader of such an opinion the problem then becomes which of these several arguments is the central point of the opinion; which of these arguments establishes the basic doctrine, rules, and principles to be relied upon and used to resolve the next dispute.)

A disagreement among the signers of an opinion is sometimes signaled when the opinion says the following: "Assuming for the sake of argument that 'X' is true, nevertheless. . . ." Or the opinion might say, "We need resolve question 'Y' to reach a decision in this case." Yet another signal occurs when the opinion says something like this: "Our analysis shows that the law would survive (be struck down) under either test."

Whatever agreements and compromises the justices reach, they minimize references or hints of such bargaining. Not to do this would be to destroy the appearance that their opinion is but an expression of, and determined by, the THE LAW. The justices want their opinion to appear as if it were entirely the product of considerations external to their personal preferences and will.

Addressing Only the Dispute before the Court

The next two points—the need to address only the dispute before the Court and the expectation that the opinion provide guidance for the future—are related. For reasons of constitutional doctrine, as well as traditional legal practice, the justices must decide only the actual dispute brought to them for review. The Supreme Court is not permitted to provide "advisory opinions" on constitutional issues that have not yet become the subject of a real dispute between real parties with something at stake; it may not provide legal advice on issues not the subject of dispute between the parties before the Court. Thus, when the justices write opinions they are expected to pay close attention to the specific issues this dispute raises. Anything they write on issues not specifically in dispute in this case will be viewed as without official legal significance, will be understood to be nothing more than their personal opinion and not official doctrine or law.

In fact, anything justices do to justify the result which subsequent judges and lawyers conclude was not truly *logically* necessary to resolving the dispute may be viewed as merely a gratuitous comment, extraneous material with virtually no legal weight (such statements are called "dictum.") A justice might, nevertheless, wish to add such comments to his or her opinion for rhetorical purposes, or perhaps in order to send a message about his or her viewpoint and attitude on a problem. While such a message is not "law," is not legally binding on the parties, and cannot be cited by other judges or lawyers as official Supreme Court doctrine, it may nevertheless serve the useful purpose of providing some guidance as to future directions the Court may take. (And gratuitous comments, "dictum," always stand a chance of becoming actual doctrine if supported in the future by at least five justices.)

This raises the question of the justices' responsibility to provide guidance to future courts, lawyers, and society in resolving problems similar in kind to the one now before the Court. The justices are expected, in resolving the specific issues before them, to do so in a way that lays down some general principles of law, some rules, some factors or guideposts which will indicate how they would approach resolving similar problems if they were to arise in the future. There is a kind of paradox at work here. Out of the specific dispute before them, the justices are expected to generate general principles, or guidelines, germane to resolving similar disputes.

Let's return to the *Brandenburg* case. The opinion would provide little guidance and assistance if the rule the Court were to announce in this case was confined to the following: "In the future Brandenburg may not be prosecuted under the Ohio syndicalism statutes when he gives a speech identical in content to the one he delivered, to an identical crowd, in the same field, and under the same circumstances." Though such a rule specifically addresses the dispute in that case, it is so specific that it is of limited future use. To provide more guidance an opinion should lead to a conclusion stated in more general terms and which can be applied or used in conjunction with a wider range of similar incidents. For example, the opinion might say the following: A speech which advocates the violent overthrow of the government in the abstract, at some indefinite point of time in the future, and which is delivered to a crowd of people indisposed to taking immediate action, is an example of speech protected by the First Amendment; such a speech may not be the subject of prosecution under criminal syndicalism statutes. (Note, however, that Brandenburg might have been prosecuted under a "disturbance of the speech" statute, but this issue was not before the Court, and any comments the Court might have made about the constitutional permissibility of prosecution under such a law would be mere dictum.)

Now, if the Court phrases the rule in a case more broadly, some readers of the opinion may argue that this general rule should be considered dictum, since such a general rule would not have been necessary to resolve the dispute. Suppose a justice were to write that the appeals court is reversed because *all* speeches advocating the violent overthrow of the government are constitutionally protected from criminal prosecution. Such a rule would resolve the dispute before the Court; it would also provide guidance for the future. But such a rule would be considerably broader than necessary to resolve this particular dispute, hence would be viewed with suspicion by future judges and lawyers. They would suspect that in fact the correctly phrased version of the rule of this case was something narrower, *despite* what actually appears in the opinion. Of course, when it is to the legal advantage of a lawyer or judge to rely on the broadly stated principles in an opinion, they will do so. It is just at this point that a dispute may arise over exactly how the opinion should be interpreted and understood. (See Chapter 5.)

Providing a Persuasive Justification

In addition to providing legal guidance for future cases, the justices need to provide a persuasive justification for the holding, rule, principle, and doctrine announced in the opinion. This means the opinion must offer a *logical* and *plausible* argument in support of the conclusion. The next chapters will go more deeply into the construction of such arguments; suffice it to say here that such an argument begins with premises or assumptions that are *plausible* or *true*, and, then, with the tools of logic moves toward the conclusion.

Again let's return to the *Brandenburg* case. The argument could begin with a discussion and analysis of precedent—prior Supreme Court opinions from which the justices extract the following premise: (1) A person may be subjected to criminal syndicalism only if his or her "advocacy is directed to inciting or producing imminent lawless action and is likely to incite or produce such action." (Assume that this rule is in fact a plausible reading of prior Supreme Court opinions.) The opinion at this point will turn to the next premise—the meaning and interpretation of this first premise. The justices will at this point discuss the first premise and conclude that it means that (1) a speech does not incite lawless action if it merely advocates the historical necessity of, to be realized at some indefinite point in the future, the violent overthrow of the government, and that there is little likelihood of imminent lawless action when such a speech is delivered to a crowd hostile to such a message.

Having established the more purely legal premises of the argument, the justices now turn to the facts of the case. After a review of the facts of the case the justices agree with Brandenburg that (2) his speech only advocated the violent overthrow of the government in the abstract, and that the crowd he addressed was not primed for immediate action.

The justices thus reach their conclusion, (3) that Brandenburg's right of freedom of speech was violated and that the conviction and opinion of the appeals court should be reversed. (Notice that this argument is in the form of a simple syllogism: (1) If "A," then "B." (2) It is the case that "A." (3) Therefore, B.)

Be forewarned that this is a particularly simple example of legal reasoning. Many opinions will require the justices to mount more complex arguments involving chains of arguments (i.e., opinions in which one argument leads to a conclusion which then serves as the premise for the next argument which leads to a conclusion, which, in turn, is used as the premise for the next argument). In addition, as we shall see in the next chapter, these linked syllogisms are used in conjunction with certain styles of justification (e.g., balancing).

The Use of the Proper Legal Materials

By now you may have detected something new about the writing of a Supreme Court opinion. The justification should be phrased in such a way that it has the appearance of being based on considerations, rules, principles, and doctrines external to the justice. The justices should present their justifications as based on THE LAW, and not based on their personal preferences and desires. The expectation, if not the reality, is that justices of the Supreme Court are discoverers and interpreters of law, not dictators imposing their personal will. This means that the tone and the style of writing used in the opinions will appear impersonal and legalistic. The justices' opinions use personal pronouns, as in the phrase "we conclude that . . . "; but such phrasing is always meant to mean, "We, acting dispassionately, disinterestedly, objectively, logically, and scientifically, conclude that the law requires us to reach this conclusion."

In building a chain of syllogisms the justices are expected to rely upon and make reference to certain kinds of "legal" materials while avoiding using or relying upon other materials. The sorts of material the justices use include the following:

1. The text of the Constitution;
2. Evidence of the intent of the framers and drafters of the Constitution;
3. Implicit premises or "tacit postulates" of the Constitution which order the relationship among the branches of the federal government, between the federal government and the states, between governments at all levels and the individual;
4. Precedent—prior opinions of the Supreme Court;
5. Evidence on American traditions, customs, and practices;
6. Evidence on contemporary morality and attitudes; and
7. Considerations of practicality and prudence.

The justices may also on occasion draw on legal commentary found in the scholarly journals, and evidence and analysis produced by social scientists. It is from these kinds of material that the justices are expected to construct the premises of their arguments.

Recall that in the argument outlined above justifying the decision in the *Brandenburg* case the materials primarily relied upon were precedent. If one were to look at this precedent itself, one would find that these opinions in turn relied on the text of the Constitution, notions of the intent of the framers, contemporary theories regarding the notion of freedom of speech, as well as yet other precedent. (Note: There are major disputes raging among the justices, lawyers, and legal philosophers over which of these materials has priority in the situation in which one set of materials points in one direction, and another set points toward a different conclusion. These disputes also include questions about how these materials are to be used and what constitutes an abuse of the materials. We shall return to these matters in Chapter 4.)

Just as there are materials the justices arguably may legitimately rely on in crafting a justification, there are certain materials which today they would be expected *not* to use: (1) bald expressions of personal preference, values, positions or personal intuition; (2) claims, for example, that God, one's parents, spouse, or the President told one what to do; (3) the Bible; (4) natural law; (5) the platform of a political party; (6) the writings of one's favorite philosopher; (7) the fact that a justice personally likes the petitioner or respondent, or feels sorry for the petitioner or respondent.

Consider how strange an opinion would sound today if such materials were used by citing examples of old opinions in which such materials were used.

> It is against all reason and justice, for a people to intrust a Legislature with such powers; and, therefore, it cannot be presumed that they have done it. *Calder v. Bull* (1798)

> I do not hesitate to declare that a state does not possess the power of revoking its own grants. But I do it on a general principle, on the reason and nature of things: a principle which will impose laws even on the Deity. *Fletcher v. Peck* (1810) (Johnson J., concurring)

> . . . we think ourselves standing upon the principles of natural justice, upon the fundamental laws of every free government, upon the spirit and letter of the Constitution of the United States. . . . *Territ v. Taylor* (1815)

In another case denying Mrs. Bradwell's application to become a lawyer the Court wrote: "[T]he civil law, as well as nature herself, has always recognized a wide difference in the respective spheres and destinies of man and woman . . . . The paramount destiny and mission of woman are to fulfill the nobel and benign offices of wife and mother. This is the law of the Creator." *Bradwell v. Illinois* (1873)(Bradley, J. concurring). And while much is said about how the justices simply act upon their personal ideology, we would be very surprised if we found a majority opinion which simply said: "We like liberalism, you like conservatism. We win, 6–3. Statute invalidated."[1]

---

[1] Cf. John Hart Ely, "Foreword: On Discovering Fundamental Values," 92 *Harv. L. Rev.* 5, 34 (1978).

Finally, in writing opinions the justices want to express positions and viewpoints on the law which are consistent with their own prior opinions, unless they have consciously changed their minds. Few things would hold a justice up to more disrepute than the production of a set of opinions expressing conflicting viewpoints—a justice's motives if not his or her very rationality would be questioned. And since the justices may expect to serve on the Court for many years, they will also want to write the opinion they're currently working on in such a way that they can live with it in the future. Now, when all five of the justices involved in writing the majority opinion have these same concerns and interests, and each justice has a different prior set of opinions which he or she has authored, it becomes even more obvious how difficult it may be to reach agreement, how much bargaining and compromising may have to occur to craft a single opinion all five of them can sign.

CONCLUSION

It may take many months for five or more justices to craft a majority opinion they all can sign. The opinion must be one they all can live with, yet it must be internally logical, coherent, and persuasive. It must have the appearance of being an inevitable conclusion based only on those materials a justice is expected to rely upon, despite the fact it is the product of considerable argument and debate. It must address only the specific questions before the Court, yet also provide guidance for the future without running so far afield as to fall into the trap of producing mere dictum. And, of course, the decision should be the "right" decision justified by reasons that are seen as sound. Being a Supreme Court justice is hard work.

CHAPTER 3

Strategies of Justification

Following the statement of facts of the case, a review of the claims and counter-claims made by the parties to the case, a summary of the decisions of the lower courts, and a statement of the issues on appeal—after all this has been done—Supreme Court opinions turn to justifying the judgment reached. It is at this point that the strategy of justification comes into play. A strategy of justification is the general approach the opinion takes to the task of justifying the judgment of the Court. And in constitutional opinion writing there are three *pure* strategies: the analogy, balancing, and deduction. These strategies can be, in turn, combined in various ways to produce several different *mixed* strategies.

THE ANALOGY

To justify a judgment by means of the analogy is a deceptively easy mode of justification. Consider the following example. Assume the Court has adopted the following rule: A state's prohibition of the importation of goods into its territory is impermissible if it is a protectionist measure, but permissible if the prohibition is directed toward legitimate local concerns. Using such a rule the Court struck down a state's barring of the importation of out of state milk; the law was designed, said the Court, to protect the state's own farmers from out of state competition. However, the Court has upheld one state's quarantine of any other states' diseased goods. Now suppose New Jersey adopts a law which prohibits the importation of solid or liquid waste which the importer seeks to dump in New Jersey. Is this law more like the invalid "milk" law or more like the valid "diseased" goods law? Which is the better analogy? In *Philadelphia v. New Jersey* (1978) the Court concluded the New Jersey law was more like the unconstitutional milk law. The solid and liquid waste, said the Court, did not pose the same immediate health threat as did diseased meat. In fact, New Jersey permitted its own solid and liquid waste to be disposed of in its landfills. The New Jersey law, concluded the Court, was an "obvious effort to saddle those outside the State with the entire burden of slowing the flow of refuse into New Jersey's remaining landfill sites."

In brief, justifying a result by way of analogy rests on the assumption that a result in case B (the case currently before the Court) can be justified by pointing to the fact that case A (the precedent) is like case B in "material" ways, and case A reached result "X," the same result as reached in case B. Stated differently, if case A and B are alike in "material" respects, then case B should be decided the same way as case A. This is true because of the maxim, "Like cases should be treated alike." And this maxim finds its force in the values of fairness and rationality (i.e., it is neither fair nor rational to treat like cases differently).

But clearly the difficult step in analogical reasoning is determining whether case B is like case A, or more like some other problem. As a practical matter no case is ever completely like another case in all respects. For example, assume that in case A a man with blue eyes robs a grocery store of three apples. Then in case B a woman with brown eyes robs a grocery store of two bananas. Are these cases alike in "material" respects, hence both should be convicted of robbery? Is the color of eyes a significant difference? Is the gender of the robbers? Is it material that one stole three apples and the other two bananas? Presumably the answer to these questions is "no." But what if the apple thief had been forced into his theft by a threat to his life, but the banana thief just did her deed for a prank? This would seem to be a relevant difference. Thus you can see that for a persuasive argument to be made on the basis of analogy, one must be convincing that the cases are analogous on the "material" facts. And making that argument successfully opens a whole new set of problems. For example, one must be prepared to say that eye color is irrelevant, but that motivation is relevant in deciding the two cases.

Now, go back to the toxic waste case—did the Court make the right comparison? Was the Court correct in saying that dumping toxic waste was not like trying to sell diseased meat—that diseased meat did raise a real issue of local concern, but that toxic waste dumping did not raise the same immediate health hazard? Is the *immediacy* of the health hazard the crucial, "material" factor that *distinguishes* the meat problem from the toxic waste problem? Is the fact that New Jersey permits its own toxic wastes to be disposed of within New Jersey material showing the absence of a real health concern? Did New Jersey have any other choice regarding its own toxic waste? Why might the Court have been correct in saying the toxic waste issue was really more like the milk case? Well, you begin to see the problems involved in using precedent. I will take up additional difficulties in using precedent in Chapter 5.

PURE BALANCING

Introduction

Opinions which rely on "balancing" take a very simple form. Roughly speaking, the opinions say, for example, that petitioner wins because we (the justices) have concluded, after weighing and balancing the interests of the petitioner and the respondent, that the interests of the petitioner are weightier. An opinion couched in this language has the appearance of being impersonal, dispassionate, and disinterested. It also has the appearance of being practical since it seems to take into account the realities faced by the contending parties. Who can say that justice was not done when the Court considered all the factors and rendered what it considered to be its best judgment regarding what is best for the individuals involved and society? Finally, this strategy is especially practical when there is no precedent available for deciding the case. That is to say, balancing can be used in cases for which there appear to be no prior relevant analogies—when the Court must confront a problem for the very first time.

The Simple Model of Pure Balancing

Pure balancing appears in a fair number of Supreme Court opinions and we shall examine an example of this strategy of justification momentarily. But, preliminarily, it is important to note that sometimes this strategy is "disguised." That is, the idea of balancing is expressed in different ways in different opinions; it will not always be stated in precisely the form which holds that one side wins because its interests outweigh the other side. It takes a bit of practice to recognize that a given justification is but a disguised version of balancing.

Let's turn to an undisguised version of balancing. The opinion might begin with an assessment of the "harm" produced by the policy. The amount or degree of harm affected by the policy can be understood as a "function of" the importance of the interests of the plaintiff times the degree of impact the policy has on those interests. Thus the opinion would address the following two points:

1. **The interests of the plaintiff.** The plaintiff could be an individual, as would be the case in an individual rights case; but the holder of these interests might also be a governmental official such as the federal district court which issued the subpoena to President Nixon in the "executive privilege case" discussed in Chapter 1 (*United States v. Nixon* [1974]).
2. **The impact on those interests of the policy being challenged.**

Next the opinion would discuss the "benefits" of the policy; these benefits would be a function of the interests the policy sought to secure and the extent to which the means chosen actually realized those interests. Hence the opinion would discuss

3. The interests which the challenged policy seeks to realize.
4. The extent to which the challenged policy actually realized those interests.

Finally, the opinion would announce its conclusion as to whether or not the harm was greater than the benefits, whether or not, on balance, the policy was constitutional.

Pure Balancing and Deferral to the Legislature

The previous section described balancing at its simplest; in other words, the strategy may take on a more complex form. In one variation on the simple model the opinion writer may announce that striking the balance is an effort best left to the judgment of the legislature, to the other branch of government; accordingly, the writer says he or she will examine the balance struck by the legislature only to determine whether that balance was reasonable. If the balance was reasonable, and even if the opinion writer himself or herself might have struck the balance differently, the Court will accept it. The writer, thus, concludes that the Court should *defer* to the judgment of the other branch of government.

Justice Frankfurter's concurring opinion in *Dennis v. United States* (1951) uses this strategy. The case involved a federal law which made it a crime to advocate knowingly the overthrow of the government or to organize a group which advocates the overthrow of the government. The petitioners challenged their convictions under the law on the grounds that the convictions violated their First Amendment right to freedom of speech. Justice Frankfurter's opinion, concurring in the judgment that the convictions be upheld, said that the primary responsibility of balancing the demands of free speech and the interest in national security belonged to Congress, and that the Court should only set aside Congress's judgment if there was no reasonable basis for it. After examining those interests the Frankfurter opinion concluded that Congress determined that the danger created by the advocacy of overthrow justified the restriction on free speech, and that it was not for the Court to second-guess the legislature.

Two Uses of Pure Balancing

Pure balancing can be used in two ways. First, it can be used simply to decide the case before the Court with the understanding that if a similar case were to arise in the future, the Court would once again balance the factors in reaching a judgment. Second, balancing can be used to arrive at a principle or rule which, when used in future cases, would not involve the Court in further balancing. Let's illustrate the use of both strategies.

In *Argersinger v. Hamlin* (1972) the question was whether indigents charged with "petty offenses" had a right to a court-appointed attorney. The majority opinion used balancing to justify its conclusion that Argersinger's constitutional rights had been denied when he was not appointed an attorney for a trial involving a minor offense, namely, carrying a concealed weapon. But then the opinion concluded by announcing the following rule: ". . . [A]bsent a knowing and intelligent waiver, no person may be imprisoned for any offense, whether classified as petty, misdemeanor, or felony unless he was represented by counsel at this trial." The concurring opinion, while agreeing that the conviction should be overturned, said that there should be no such absolute rule, that balancing should be used in each and every future case to determine whether the accused should be provided with a court-appointed lawyer. The concurrence then concluded with a sketch of the factors that should be weighed in these future cases.

Problems in Using Pure Balancing

Let's now return to problems involved in the writing of a justification using balancing. It is difficult for an opinion writer to provide an accurate and precise comparative assessment of the harms and benefits involved in a case because there is usually no common unit of measure in which to carry out the comparison (e.g., harms are worth $352 and benefits are worth $353). This means that sometimes the opinions do little more than fully describe the interests at stake in colorful and persuasive terms. Justice Frankfurter, for example, in the concurring opinion discussed above, simply analyzed the government's interests by describing at great length the size, organization, and threat posed by the Communist Party. Opinions may resort to a mere listing of the interests at stake on each side. Or the opinion writer may try indirectly to get at the importance of the interests by citing analogies. Thus, in a case questioning the constitutionality of involuntary "stomach pumping" (vomiting induced with an emetic agent) undertaken to recover capsules the petitioner had swallowed, Justice Frankfurter wrote that this method of criminal investigation was "too close to the rack and screw to permit of constitutional differentiation" (*Rochin v. California* [1952]).

The use of the analogy to help pinpoint the importance, or lack of importance, of an interest is, however, tricky. As you know, analogies are never perfect. Is "stomach pumping" really like the rack and screw? Take another example. In *Wyman v. James* (1971) the Court considered whether or not a visit by a caseworker to the home of a welfare recipient was constitutionally permissible in the absence of a search warrant. Citing the text of the Fourth Amendment and precedent, the majority opinion emphasized the importance of privacy of the home. Yet, the opinion also invoked an *analogy*. The home visit, wrote the Court, was "akin" to the routine civil audits conducted by the Internal Revenue Service. This home visit was as administratively necessary as the audit, and both invaded a sphere of privacy. Yet if those audits could be constitutionally required, so could this visit. The opinion concluded that the home visit was a reasonable administrative tool; it served valid purposes and was not an unwarranted invasion of personal privacy.

But an astute reader of this opinion would ask whether a visit in someone's home is really the same thing as looking at business records? Has not the home been traditionally considered a private sanctuary? Does it not have a status never accorded to mere business records? These rhetorical questions are meant to have only one answer; thus the critic might say that the Court offered an unconvincing argument in support of its judgment.

How strong a state's interest is in its policy may be indirectly assessed by looking at the number of other states pursuing the same policy. If many states do the same thing, the interest is strong; if many do not, the interest is less. Assessment of interests may take the opinion writer into a detailed examination of tradition, especially tradition embodied in the common law and other official policies. Thus, in *Tennessee v. Garner* (1985), in considering whether it was constitutional for the police to use deadly force to stop a fleeing and unarmed criminal suspect, the Court looked to police practices generally, the old English common law rules on the matter, the modern trend in state law on the question, the modern trend in police policy around the country, and statistical data on the effect of crime rates when the police have followed a policy of limited use of deadly force.

Besides the problem of providing a precise assessment of the interests, opinion writers face the difficulty of how to describe them. Take the Communist conspiracy case again. Is this a conflict between (a) the interest of individuals to be left alone, to live their own lives and speak their own minds, as opposed to (b) the interest of the state to suppress extreme political opinions? Or did that case involve (c) a conflict between the interest of individuals to advocate false and misleading and immoral doctrines and (d) the interest of those in power to suppress political dissent in order to protect their political base? Or perhaps the conflict should be described as one between (a) and (d), or between (b) and (c). Thus, for a legal argument to be persuasive it must use descriptions of the interests which are plausible, which seem to capture what really is at stake in the dispute.

A criticism which has been made of balancing is that it is so flexible and adaptive a strategy that the justices can use it to justify any conclusion they prefer for purely personal and subjective reasons. In the "stomach pumping" case noted above Justice Frankfurter relied on an investigation of "the decencies of civilized conduct" as part of his assessment of the interests at stake. Justice Black, who agreed that stomach pumping was unconstitutional, disagreed with Frankfurter's strategy of justification. He demanded, "[W]hat avenues of investigation are open to discover 'canons' of conduct so universally favored that this Court should write them into the Constitution?"

PURE DEDUCTION

Deduction in Action

Supreme Court opinions use deduction far more frequently than balancing. The justices use deduction in conjunction with almost all the constitutional problems discussed in Chapter 1. There are, in fact, so many examples of pure deduction that it is difficult to choose among them in order to illustrate their use. But perhaps a good way to demonstrate the use of this mode of justification is to look at three opinions reflective of two different ideological perspectives, but all using deduction. *You should note that I have simplified and made clear the essence of the argument in these opinions. When you confront the actual opinions—either in edited or unedited form—the deductive argument will not be so plain. It will take some digging to uncover the premises, to sort them in the right order, to see which paragraphs serve as proofs for which premises. Supreme Court opinions can appear, at first, as somewhat disorganized. It is the reader's task to uncover the order beneath the seeming chaos.*

The dispute in *Munn v. Illinois* (1877) involved a claim that a state law which set the maximum fee a private warehouse could charge for the storage of grain was unconstitutional because, among other reasons, it violated the Fourteenth Amendment's prohibition that states not deprive persons of life, liberty, or property without due process of law. The Court upheld the regulation against this and all the other challenges. The opinion justified this conclusion in the following way:

(a) *Premise*: The text of the Constitution prohibits the "deprivation" of property.
   Proof: This point was easily established since it required nothing more than a direct quotation of the text of the Fourteenth Amendment.

(b) *Premise*: There is no "deprivation" of property when government regulates the use of property for the public good.
   Proof: 1. When one becomes a member of society one necessarily parts with some rights and privileges.

   2. The body politic is a social compact through which people agree that they shall be governed by certain laws for the common good. This means people authorize government to pass laws which require citizens to use their property so as not unnecessarily to injure another.

   3. Regulation of a variety of businesses has been a custom in English law from time immemorial, and in this country from its first colonization. In 1820 only a few decades after the adoption of the Fifth Amendment, which contains the same due process clause as in the Fourteenth, Congress passed a law which regulated the rate of wharfage at private wharves, and an 1848 law regulated the rates of hauling by cartmen and others.

4. Thus, it is apparent that down to the time of the adoption of the Fourteenth Amendment, "it was not supposed that statutes regulating the use, or even the price of the use, of private property necessarily deprived an owner of his property without due process of law."

[*Note*: this line of argument presupposes the premise that in interpreting the Constitution it is the "original intent of the framers" which is the best evidence of the meaning of the text.]

(c) *Premise*: The power of regulating property for the public good extends to the regulation of property "affected with the public interest."

Proof: The common law, from which the right to property derives, recognized that property "affected with the public interest" may be subject to public regulation. Property devoted to use in which the public has an interest becomes affected with the public interest.

(d) *Premise and Conclusion*: Public grain warehouses are "affected with the public interest," therefore they may be regulated.

Proof: If cartmen, the wharfinger, and other business regulated in the past are affected with the public interest, so is this warehouse. And we must assume that "if a state of facts could exist that would justify such legislation, it actually did exist when the statute now under consideration was passed. . . . Of the propriety of legislative interference within the scope of legislative power, the legislature is the exclusive judge."

Note the materials the Court used in constructing its argument: text, political philosophy, traditional practices, analogy, and a principle of deference to the legislature.

Forty-six years later the Court reached a very different conclusion, but the strategy of justification was the same, deduction. Challenged in *Adkins v. Children's Hospital* (1923) was a federal law authorizing a board in the District of Columbia to set minimum wages for women and minors. In striking down the law as a violation of the same due process clause involved in the previous opinion, the Court offered the following justification:

(a) *Premise*: The right to liberty protected by the Fourteenth Amendment includes an implied right to freedom of contract.

Proof: The opinion based this proposition upon precedent. Freedom of contract is not expressly mentioned in the constitutional text, but prior opinions had concluded there is such an implied right.

(b) *Premise*: This law infringes freedom of contract (an implicit assumption of the opinion).

(c) *Premise*: Freedom of contract may be infringed only if justified by the existence of exceptional circumstances.

Proof: No specific support is offered for this proposition at the point in the opinion in which it is announced. But elsewhere in the opinion the Court makes reference to how the good of society is served by the preservation of liberty. Precedent might also have been used to support the great weight the Court attaches to freedom of contract.

(d) *Premise*: The exceptional circumstances necessary to justify infringement of freedom of contract do not exist in this case.

Proof: The opinion examined a series of arguments offered to justify the law, and rejected each one.

1. The opinion rejected an argument from analogy, namely, that this regulation was similar to other minimum wage regulations which the Court in previous cases had upheld.

2. The opinion brushed aside the point that several states had adopted similar legislation. The validity of the law could not be determined "by counting heads."

3. The opinion rejected evidence that such minimum wage laws had improved the earnings of women. The improvements "may be, and quite probably are, due to other causes. . . ."

4. The opinion rejected the claim that the law served social justice. "To sustain the individual freedom of action contemplated by the Constitution, is not to strike down the common good, but to exalt it; for surely the good of society as a whole cannot be better served than by the preservation against arbitrary restraint of the liberties of its constituent members."

Then in the midst of these passages (points 1 through 4) the opinion interjected an additional and separate argument.

Premise: This law violates the Constitution because it is a naked, arbitrary exercise of power.

Proof: The argument for this conclusion is best directly quoted.

> The feature of this statute which, perhaps more than any other, puts upon it the stamp of invalidity is that it exacts from the employer an arbitrary payment for a purpose and upon a basis having no causal connection with his business, or the contract or the work the employee engages to do. . . . The ethical right of every worker, man or woman, to a living wage may be conceded. . . . [B]ut the fallacy of the proposed method of attaining it is that it assumes that every employer is bound at all events to furnish it. The moral requirement implicit in every contract of employment, viz., that the amount to be paid and the service to be rendered shall bear to each other some relation of just equivalence, is completely ignored. . . . Certainly the employer by paying a fair equivalent for the service rendered, though not sufficient to support the employee, has neither caused nor contributed to her poverty. On the contrary, to the extent of what he pays he has relieved it. In principle, there can be no difference between the case of selling labor and the case of selling goods. If one goes to the butcher, the baker or grocer to buy food, he is morally entitled to obtain the worth of his money but he is not entitled to more. If what he gets is worth what he pays he is

not justified in demanding more simply because he needs more; and the shopkeeper, having dealt fairly and honestly in that transaction, is not concerned in any peculiar sense with the question of his customer's necessities. . . .

Fourteen years after the decision in *Adkins* the Court reversed itself and overturned *Adkins* in *West Coast Hotel Co. v. Parrish* (1937). The opinion questioned the existence of the implied right to freedom of contract. Relying on an argument reminiscent of the political theory used in point (b) in the *Munn* case discussed above, the opinion stressed that the "liberty" protected by the Constitution was not absolute. In an implied attack on the last argument of the *Adkins* opinion the Court said it could be assumed the "minimum wage is fixed in consideration of the services that are performed. . . ." The opinion quoted with approval Chief Justice Taft's comment that the minimum wage would only have the effect of cutting into the profits of business wrung from their employees. It noted the social good that would be done by the law—it would reduce "exploiting workers at wages so low as to be insufficient to meet the bare costs of living, thus, making their very helplessness the occasion of a most injurious competition." The opinion used a "head count" of other states to show the importance of these laws and their presumed value. It noted the unparalleled demands for relief during the Depression. And it concluded by saying, "The Community is not bound to provide what is in effect a subsidy for unconscionable employers. The community may direct its law-making power to correct the abuse which springs from their selfish disregard of the public interest. . . ."

Deduction and the Illusion of Certainty

Justification through use of a deductive argument is obviously a powerful tool of persuasion. But it should now be clear that it is a tool that can be used to justify many different positions. The key to the effort is the premises and the providing of proof for those premises. Note that the effort of providing proof of the premises may *not* be an exercise in pure deduction. Look again at the last argument of the *Adkins* opinion. It contains a bald unsupported assertion: "The moral requirement implicit in every contract of employment, viz., that the amount to be paid and the service to be rendered shall bear to each other some relation of just equivalence is completely ignored. . . ." It relies on an analogy: "In principle, there can be no difference between the case of selling labor and the case of selling goods." And though the opinion adopted this analogy, it also denied that there was any analogy between the law in this case and those other minimum wage laws protecting women which were upheld in prior Supreme Court opinions.

Also recall that *Adkins* used precedent to support the conclusion that there was a constitutional right to freedom of contract. That conclusion probably was a fair reading of the precedent. But sometimes precedent is subject to multiple and conflicting interpretations (see Chapter 5); thus using precedent to establish premises can be a tricky exercise. In any event, what if the precedent you rely on was itself incorrectly decided? The *Parrish* opinion attacks the precedent in *Adkins* when it questions the existence of a constitutional right to freedom of contract. In short, deduction is a powerful tool but it requires skill, art, and judgment in order to use it well. The argument may be *logical*, but is it *plausible*? Are the premises well grounded?

Digging Out the Argument

The above summaries of *Munn*, *Adkins*, and *Parrish* "cleaned up" and made clearer the arguments of those opinions. In the original opinions the basic structure of the arguments is not so evident. Supreme Court opinions are not written with the *premises* and *proofs* labeled as such. The reader must determine for him- or herself which of the many sentences are the premises, which of the paragraphs are the proofs.

One may also have to "restructure" the opinion to make it clear. The material in the fourth paragraph of the opinion may in fact contain the premise for which the first three paragraphs provide the proof. And sometimes, as we saw in *Adkins*, there may be implicit or unstated premises at work. *Adkins* also illustrates how an argument may be jumbled: The opinion contained a logically separate and distinct argument inserted between paragraphs addressed to a different argument. In sum, opinions, especially in their unedited versions, can be unruly, complex affairs in which it seems the thread of the argument has been lost as the opinion takes up seemingly extraneous points, rebuts arguments it disagrees with, and explores precedent.

MIXED STRATEGIES

Because a judicial opinion is expected to provide general guidance for the future, it is common for an opinion to use balancing or deduction to lead up to the announcement of a rule, test, or standard of review. Having announced such a rule, these opinions turn to the application of that rule, test, or standard of review to reach a conclusion. These rules or tests may themselves require either balancing or deduction. Thus, there are, roughly speaking, four types of opinions: (1) those opinions that use deduction to produce a test or rule which is then applied through deduction, (2) those opinions which use deduction to produce a test or rule which in turn requires balancing to resolve the dispute, (3) opinions which begin with balancing to produce a test or rule which is applied deductively, and (4) opinions which start with balancing and lead to a test or rule that itself requires further balancing.

Deduction Plus Deduction

In *Carter v. Carter Coal Co.* (1936) the Court was asked to resolve a dispute over the constitutionality of a complex piece of federal legislation which, roughly speaking, regulated coal mining in various ways. In simple terms, the issue was whether Congress's explicit grant of authority to regulate interstate commerce gave it the power to regulate such aspects of the mining industry as the wages paid workers, and the hours they worked. In one of those complex, long, and unruly the opinions that the Court can produce, we can—with some digging—uncover the following argument:

First Deduction

1. The intent of the framers was to preserve unimpaired state self-government in all matters not committed to the general government.
2. Every addition to the national legislative power detracts from or invades the power of the states.
3. In order to maintain the fixed balance between federal government and states, the powers of the federal government should not be so extended as to embrace any not within the express terms of the several grants or implications necessarily to be drawn from them.
4. The validity of the law depends on whether it is a regulation of "interstate *commerce*," the phrase used in the Constitution.
5. In light of points 1–3, the term "commerce" should be narrowly interpreted. (This is an implicit premise/conclusion of the opinion.)
6. Turning then to the definition of the term "commerce," this word means "intercourse for the purpose of *trade*" and does *not* embrace employment of men, fixing of wages and hours; these latter activities are intercourse for purposes of *production* and not for *trade*. Mining itself merely brings the subject matter of commerce into existence. It is commerce which disposes of it.
7. For this law to be constitutional it must regulate "commerce" and not "production." (This is the test developed by the opinion.)

Second Deduction

8. Applying this test we conclude that this law regulates *production*, not trade or commerce.

Conclusion

Therefore, this law is unconstitutional.

Now consider the Court's decision in *Brown v. Board of Education* (1954) in which the Court said that the purposeful segregation of students by race by law in the public schools was unconstitutional. This is an equal protection case in which students were classified by race. In the first part of the opinion the Court discussed the original intent of the equal protection clause of the Fourteenth Amendment and concluded that the amendment's history was inconclusive on the question of whether public school segregation was unconstitutional. Then, turning to precedent, the Court *deduced* that precedent established that "separate but equal" facilities were permissible as long as those facilities were equal both in their tangible and intangible features. Thus, the Court went on to determine (the second deduction) whether or not the "separate but equal" test as properly interpreted had been satisfied. The opinion concluded that it had not, and that, in fact, it could never be satisfied in the field of public education. "Separate educational facilities are inherently unequal." The precise basis of this conclusion is a matter of considerable controversy—was it the psychological and other materials cited in footnote 11, or was this conclusion based on the common-sensical observation that forced segregation stigmatizes the minority and cannot, therefore, but be harmful? Whatever the answer is to this particular question, note that often the application of tests and standards of review can involve the use of complex pieces of research and data which themselves may be the subject of controversy and conflicting interpretations.

A third example of deduction plus deduction comes from those opinions which rely on the *rational basis test* (both the equal protection and substantive due process versions). (See Chapter 1, pp. 18, 23.) These opinions discuss the meaning of the due process or equal protection clauses of the Fourteenth Amendment, reflect upon the proper role of the Court in relation to the legislature, specifically the appropriateness of the Court *deferring* to the legislative judgment. ("We have returned to the original constitutional proposition that courts do not substitute their social and economic beliefs for the judgment of legislative bodies, who are elected to pass laws" *Ferguson v. Skrupa* [1963].) Based on these considerations the opinion deduces the rational basis test which, as I have discussed, is very deferential toward the legislature. The opinion then moves on to apply the test to the problem at hand: Has the plaintiff shown that the law does *not* serve a legitimate purpose? Or has the plaintiff shown that the law is *not* rationally related to that purpose?

Looking back at these three examples you will see that the first deduction can be begun by reliance on a wide range of legal materials (e.g., intent of the framers, the constitutional text, precedent, etc.). The second deduction, in turn, involves taking the rule or test developed in the first deduction and employing it in a follow-up syllogism. For example, look at step 8 of *Carter Coal*. This step can be elaborated in the following way: (a) Congress may regulate "commerce," but it may not regulate "production." (b) Mining coal is production, not commerce. (c) Therefore, this law is unconstitutional.

Deduction Plus Balancing

Here is a controversial example of a deduction that leads to balancing. The controversy surrounds the Court's deduction of the strict scrutiny test.[1] The Court said that when fundamental rights have been affected by government's policy, or government used a "suspect" classification (criterion), then "strict scrutiny of the classification which the state makes . . . is essential, lest unwittingly, or otherwise, invidious discriminations are made against groups or types of individuals in violation of the constitutional guaranty of just and equal laws" (*Skinner v. Oklahoma* [1942]).

The controversy over this deduction focuses on the question of why the Court selected the strict scrutiny test. Never really explained in this deduction is why some other somewhat less stringent test should not be used in cases touching on a fundamental interest or involving government's use of a suspect classification. For example, the Court could as easily have said that the appropriate test is one that states government's policy is only constitutional "if it serves an important purpose, and the means in fact serve in a real way the realization of that end."

But the Court omitted making the link between fundamental interests and suspect classifications and leapt to the strict scrutiny test. Turning to that test, if one looks at it closely one could see it as embodying a disguised form of balancing. In other words, the test involves the Court in discussing, given the great importance of the individual interest at stake, or the suspect nature of the classification, whether or not the reasons for this law are strong enough to justify the invasion of the interest, the imposition of a harm. That is to say, a case like *Skinner* says when the individual interests at risk are really important (i.e., a fundamental interest), then government's policy is only constitutional if it effectively serves a purpose so important that these purposes outweigh the possible harm.

Let's look at a specific example. After the Japanese bombing of Pearl Harbor and the declaration of war on Japan, the federal government ordered the exclusion of all people of Japanese ancestry from the West Coast and the relocation of them in special camps scattered around the country (*Korematsu v. United States* [1944]). In reviewing this classification based on racial ancestry, the majority opinion noted that "[A]ll restrictions which curtail the civil rights of a single racial group are immediately suspect. That is not to say that all such restrictions are unconstitutional. It is to say the courts must subject them to the most rigid scrutiny." (The background to this statement was a long history of racial discrimination in the United States. Laws which drew a distinction among people on the basis of race are "suspect" because there is a high probability the

---

[1] Recall that when this test is used it is the government which must carry the burden of proof to prevent the law from being struck down. Government must establish that the law is necessary to the achievement of a purpose which is compelling.

actual basis of the law was racial prejudice, not sound public policy.) The opinion then continued in a balancing mode by considering both the harm done to these U.S. citizens of Japanese ancestry who were removed from their homes and property, and the national security interests of the United States. The Court concluded that the need to reduce all possible risks of sabotage and espionage in wartime justified this extraordinary infringement of civil rights.

Balancing Plus Deduction

Balancing followed by deduction characterizes many areas of constitutional law. One of the clearest examples of this mode of justification is to be found in *New York v. Ferber* (1982). At issue was a New York statute prohibiting the distribution of materials depicting children under 16 engaged in sexual conduct regardless of whether the materials were "obscene" according to the technical definition of obscenity developed by the Supreme Court. The opinion reviewed the costs associated with the production of such materials (impact on the child's psychological and physical well being); the benefits of child pornography (exceedingly modest, if not de minimis); and the law's effectiveness in reducing the production of such materials (prohibiting distribution was the most expeditious if not the only practical way to protect children (it dries up the market for these materials). Based on this *balance* the opinion concluded that child pornography should be placed outside the protection of the First Amendment. Then, the opinion went on to say that any law banning this material, in order to be constitutional, must meet certain tests: The law may only ban visual depictions of a specified act of sexual conduct of children, and the term "sexual conduct" must be suitably limited and described. However, the prohibited depiction need not be limited to that which is patently offensive; nor need it be limited to only that material which appeals to the prurient interest; and the material at issue need not be evaluated as a whole. Using these tests the Court concluded (*deduced*) that New York's law was constitutional.

Balancing Plus Balancing

The opinions which use this strategy of justification engage in balancing in order to produce a test which itself calls for the further balancing of factors specified in the test. We have already seen an example of such an opinion earlier in this chapter, the concurring opinion in *Argersinger v. Hamlin* (1972) dealing with the right to an attorney for trials for petty criminal offenses. Consider another example from the Court's opinions on freedom of speech. The question arose in *Connick v. Myers* (1983) and *Pickering v. Board of Education* (1968) whether or not citizens continue to enjoy their First Amendment free speech rights to criticize the government when they become employees of that same government.

In resolving the question the Court's opinions have balanced, on the one hand, the interest of the individual to speak out, the public's interest in learning what the employee has to say, and, on the other hand, the interests of the public in the continued smooth operation of the government. The balancing of these considerations led the Court to the following test: If the employee spoke out truthfully on a matter of "public concern" (itself a term that the Court has spent some effort in defining), then the speech activity may only be the subject of disciplinary action after weighing the following factors—the impact of the speech on working relations with fellow employees, the impact on the working relationship with the immediate superior, and how serious or fundamental were the issues raised by the employee.

JUDICIAL DISAGREEMENTS

Disagreements among the justices over the results in a particular case are often argued using differing strategies of justification. Take for example the majority and dissenting opinions in *Panhandle Oil Co. v. Truax* (1928). At issue was the constitutionality of a Mississippi law which imposed on gasoline dealers a tax of 1 cent per gallon sold for the privilege of engaging in business. A gasoline dealer who sold gas to the U.S. Coast Guard and a Veterans Hospital refused to pay the tax claiming it was an unconstitutional tax on the federal government itself. A majority of the Court, in an opinion authored by Justice Butler, concluded that the tax was unconstitutional; it justified its conclusion using a pure deductive argument. A dissenting opinion authored by Justice Holmes, which would have upheld the tax, relied on pure balancing. Here is a rough summary of each opinion.

Justice Butler for the Majority
Precedent establishes that state may not burden or interfere with the exertion of national power by taxing the means used for the performance of federal functions. This tax falls on the transaction or sale, and its size depends on the quantity purchased. As such, this tax must inevitably retard the amount purchased. Thus, the necessary effect of the tax is directly to retard, impede, and burden the exertion of the United States of its constitutional power to operate the fleet and hospital. Thus this is an unconstitutional tax; the petitioner is not liable for the taxes.

Justice Holmes for Justices Brandeis and Stone
The question of state interference with the federal government is one of reasonableness and degree. This is a reasonable tax in that it only asks of the federal government that it help pay for the state services it uses just as every other business or person must. The federal government has itself not complained about the tax. We have never said that sales taxes on the food and clothing the federal government purchases are unconstitutional. And as long as

this Court sits it can determine which tax is confiscatory. This tax is reasonable in its purpose; it has only a remote effect on the federal government.

Reliance on different strategies of justification is not the only way majority, dissenting, and concurring opinions may differ. Whether using the same or a different strategy, these opinions may rely upon and work with different constitutional materials. Thus the majority opinion may stress deduction based on precedent, while the dissent may stress deduction based on the original intent of the framers. The next chapter will take up conflicts over the use of these other legal materials.

CONCLUSION

This chapter described seven strategies of justification. These materials will provide a starting point for appreciating the reasoning of Supreme Court opinions. But note that some opinions may not be so easily classified. This may be true for several reasons. Some opinions involve many different kinds of constitutional challenges that cannot be placed in any one of our categories (e.g., both due process and equal protection challenges). A few other opinions, although dealing with a single challenge, may involve balancing in conjunction with deduction to arrive at a test which is then applied deductively. A small number of other opinions which in fact fit our categories may also bristle with so many subsidiary issues that they may not appear to fit. And a few other opinions simply cannot be fitted into our categories without some distortion, e.g., those opinions dealing with the scope of the authority of the federal courts to develop and impose desegregation plans on school districts.

Even as to those many opinions which easily fit our categories, one may discover that they do not march up as neatly ranked as I have made them appear. Finding the justification strategies, seeing how analogies are used, and discovering the underlying set of linked syllogisms takes work. But going through this exercise is an important part of what it means to study and interpret a constitutional opinion. And different people may arrive at different understandings of the opinions. This conflict in views over the interpretation of opinions is a marked feature of a life within the law. If there were no such disagreements, think how many fewer legal disputes and court decisions there would be.

AFTERWORD: STRATEGIES OF JUSTIFICATION

The broadly sketched picture of the strategies of justification can be refined and further illuminated in a number of respects. This addendum begins with the problem of classification. It then turns to the link between, on the one hand, balancing and deduction, and, on the other hand, analogy.

Classification

It is frequently the case in opinion writing that the author must decide whether a particular event, activity, policy, or thing is covered by a phrase that actually appears in the Constitution, or covered by a rule, test, or standard of review developed in precedent. For example, opinions have wrestled with whether sleeping in a park is, or could be classified as, a form of "speech"; whether a sniff by a dog of the air surrounding luggage is a "search" of that luggage; whether a job with a public employer is a species of "property"; whether a particular publication is "obscene"; whether a particular activity poses a "clear and present danger of imminent lawless action"; whether a government's policy serves a purpose which is "legitimate," and/or "compelling," etc.

These questions raise the problem of *labeling* or *classifying*. A persuasive opinion must offer reasons why it does or does not impose a particular label, does or does not classify something.

Consider the question of whether a Negro slave brought into a free state was a "United States citizen" who was entitled to bring suit in a federal court (*Dred Scott v. Sandford* [1857]). The opinion used an approach to constitutional interpretation that relied heavily upon the "intent of the framers." Hence, the opinion reviewed English and American attitudes toward the Negro before and at the time of the adoption of the Constitution; it also examined the text of the Constitution itself and concluded that the answer was "no." Dred Scott was not a citizen. Note the syllogism in this argument: (1) The Constitution's meaning is determined by the intent of the framers. (2) The intent of the framers was that Negro slaves were not to be considered citizens of the United States and could not be made citizens by the action of an individual state. (3) Dred Scott is a Negro slave who claims to have become a citizen by having traveled in a free state. (4) Scott's claim is inconsistent with the Constitution. Therefore, Scott is not a citizen of the United States and may not bring this suit.

The Analogy, Balancing, and Deduction

We have already seen how balancing and deduction can be combined in one overall argument. Analogy can also be used in conjunction with the strategies of balancing and deduction. Take for example a deductive argument. For the argument to proceed, it is necessary to select the starting premise. Finding this premise may require the use of an analogy. Take the problem of whether sleeping in the park to demonstrate the plight of the homeless is a form of "speech." The opinion writer might seek to compare this kind of activity with picketing, an activity acknowledged to be a form of "speech" activity. Thus the question arises whether sleeping in the park is sufficiently like picketing as also to be called a "speech" activity. If the answer is "yes," then the park-sleeping case should be decided using the tests, rules, doctrines, and principles taken from the picketing case. The deduction can then begin.

Here is another example. Consider one of tests used in cases in which governmental assistance to private religious schools is challenged as a violation of the establishment clause of the First Amendment. (The establishment clause, let's say, prohibits most forms of governmental assistance to religion.) The test states that the primary effect of the aid must not be to advance or inhibit religion (first premise). Thus, the opinion must resolve the question of whether or not the aid advances or inhibits religion. To help in reaching this conclusion the opinion may consider analogies. Suppose that in a prior opinion that Court had concluded that lending textbooks directly to *students* attending private religious schools was permissible (did not advance religion). Also suppose the Court had held that the loan of wall maps to those same students did advance religion, thus was impermissible. Now suppose the aid took the form of a book of maps (an atlas). Is this an impermissible form of aid? Classifying the atlas would involve a comparison between wall maps and textbooks.

CHAPTER 4

The Legal Materials Used in Building a Constitutional Justification

This chapter turns to the use of the legal materials that must be employed in conjunction with the strategies of justification. For example, the strategy of deduction must begin with a premise. This premise must be grounded in something, namely, appropriate legal materials such as the text of the Constitution, the intent of the framers, or precedent. It follows that in order fully to understand a constitutional opinion one needs to pay close attention to an opinion's use of these materials.

The materials in question are

1. The text of the Constitution;
2. Evidence of the intent of the framers and drafters of the Constitution;
3. Implicit premises or "tacit postulates" of the Constitution which order the relationship among the branches of the federal government, between the federal government and the states, and between government and the individual;
4. Precedent—prior opinions of the Supreme Court;
5. Evidence on American traditions, customs, and practices;
6. Evidence on contemporary morality and attitudes; and
7. Considerations of practicality and prudence.

To begin, it is useful to draw a distinction between two types of constitutional problem. First are those problems which arise in the absence of any precedent, and second are those which arise against a background of previous Supreme Court opinions. Problems of the first kind obviously can draw only on materials

(1) through (3) and (5) to (7); it is problems of this kind which this chapter takes up. Chapter 5 will discuss the use of precedent in the crafting of a justification of a constitutional decision.

Having drawn this sharp distinction, I want now to blur it by noting that sometimes it is useful, even if a problem arises against a background of existing precedent, to treat it *as if* the case were without precedent. Thus, opinion writers may write their opinions by dealing with the problem before them *as if* there were no precedent, and then, having looked at the problem in this way, they may turn to providing a separate justification in terms of precedent.

There are four issues surrounding the use of constitutional materials other than precedent.

1. *What materials may properly be used by the justices in forging a justification for a constitutional decision?*

   Should or may the justices rely on materials external to the Constitution and not considered by the drafters? For example, may the justices rely on contemporary morality as a basis for interpreting the Constitution?

2. *How may a particular set of materials be used?*

   For example, should the text of the Constitution be read literally? When the First Amendment states that Congress shall make "no law" abridging freedom of speech, should that be understood to mean that even "crying fire in a crowded theater" may *not* be prohibited?

3. *What is the proper method of gathering the relevant evidence?*

   How should the justices determine the intent of the framers? How are the justices to uncover tradition? the principles of contemporary morality?

4. *What priority ranking should these materials be given?*

   Take the example of a conflict between the text of the Constitution and evidence of the intent of the framers such that the text seems to support one conclusion and evidence of intent a different conclusion. In this situation, which set of materials is to control the interpretation of the Constitution? Here is a famous example of such a conflict. Looking at the First Amendment we see that the text says "no law" abridging speech may be adopted, yet there is evidence the framers intended to bar only certain laws affecting free speech, laws which imposed prior restraints on free speech, e.g., by requiring newspapers to get a governmental license before they could publish. In this situation which material has the higher priority?

This chapter explores these questions by focusing on the answers the justices have provided to them and through review of the positions legal scholars have taken on these same issues.

FOUR APPROACHES TO THE USE OF LEGAL MATERIALS

The debate among the justices and legal scholars over the use of legal materials is a four-sided debate that can best be visualized with a matrix (below).

	Originalism (Interpretism)	Nonoriginalism (Noninterpretism)
Judicial Activism		
Judicial Restraint		

Put most simply, interpretism or originalism holds that a law, policy, or other governmental action is unconstitutional only if the original beliefs of the ratifiers of the constitutional text entail the conclusion that government has done something it may not do. That is, originalism requires a justice to rely on the text of the Constitution and the original beliefs of the ratifiers (as well as precedent that also was based on such an approach.)[1]

For the noninterpretist or nonoriginalist the original meaning of the text is not the only meaning. The noninterpretist thinks the constitutional text can have multiple meanings and it is legitimate to turn to other legal materials, tradition, contemporary morality, to determine the best meaning.

Let's turn now from the concepts of originalism and nonoriginalism, to the notions of restraint and activism. Judicial restraint holds that the Court should approach its work fully cognizant of the facts that (1) the Court is not an elected body; (2) the other branches of the government are often elected and, at least in the case of the federal government, co-equal with the Supreme Court; and (3) the Court lacks certain institutional capacities enjoyed by the other branches. Thus, a proponent of judicial restraint advocates that the Court should use its power of judicial review with restraint; it should defer to the other branches of government; and it should only strike down as unconstitutional the laws, policies, and actions of the other branches when the constitutional violation is too plain to be doubted.

Judicial activists acknowledge the points (1)–(3) made by the advocates of restraint, but go on to note that the Court has been assigned special roles in the constitutional scheme that cannot be adequately fulfilled by judicial inaction.

---

[1] Michael J. Perry, *Morality, Politics and Law* (New York: Oxford University Press, 1988), p. 125.

Judicial passivity opens the door to a variety of constitutional transgressions; it is the obligation of the Court to use its powers and not abdicate its responsibilities to protect, for example, individual rights.

When these four concepts are combined to form the matrix, we end up with four approaches to constitutional adjudication: (1) originalism and activism; (2) originalism and restraint; (3) nonoriginalism and activism; and (4) nonoriginalism and restraint. As will be demonstrated in this chapter, many of the justices of the Supreme Court can be located in one of these four categories. But you should be forewarned that the justices are not philosophers who develop wholly internally consistent and coherent philosophies. The justices are caught in the realities of a world of conflicting pressures and concerns; in addition, the justices are not above pursuing a political agenda even if that means abandoning a consistent approach to judicial craftsmanship. Thus, it is rare to find a justice who is always, in every case, for example, an originalist who acts with restraint. Indeed, arguably the greatest justice ever to sit on the Supreme Court, Chief Justice John Marshall, was both an nonoriginalist who acted with restraint in some cases, and an originalist who adopted an activist posture in others (see Opinions of Chief Justice Marshall: An Addendum to this chapter).

FORMS OF ORIGINALISM

Introduction

Nobody questions that the text of the Constitution itself may be used in the crafting of a Supreme Court opinion. The central question has been, "How is the text to be dealt with?" One approach to the use of the text is literalism, an approach which says that when the words of the Constitution have a plain meaning, that meaning must be followed regardless of any unfortunate consequences. But few people take this approach to the Constitution seriously. "If simply *reading* the Constitution the "right" way were all the justices of the Supreme Court had to do, the only qualification for the job would be literacy, and the only tool a dictionary."[2] Thus, the approach which has gained favor is "originalism."

Explicit statements in support of originalism appear in almost all time periods. An early endorsement of originalism appeared in 1838 when the Court wrote, "The solution of this question must necessarily depend on the words of the Constitution; the meaning and intention of the convention which framed and proposed it for adoption and ratification to the conventions . . . in the several states, . . . together with reference to such sources of judicial information as

---

[2]Lawrence H. Tribe, *God Save this Honorable Court* (New York: Mentor, 1985), pp. 50–51.

are resorted to by all courts in construing statutes, and to which this Court has always resorted in construing the Constitution" (*Rhode Island v. Massachusetts* [1838]). In 1925 the Court wrote that "The Fourth Amendment is to be construed in light of what was deemed an unreasonable search and seizure when it was adopted . . ." (*Carroll v. United States* [1925]). Justice Harlan, himself not a very consistent originalist, issued one of the most forceful statements of originalism in 1970: "When the Court disregards the express intent and understanding of the framers, it has invaded the realm of the political process to which the amending power is committed, and it has violated the constitutional structure which it is its highest duty to protect" (*Oregon v. Mitchell* [1970] [Harlan, J., concurring in part and dissenting in part]).

Originalism has its roots in a strict notion of the rule of law which itself rests on an important insight: a government strong enough to carry out its required functions can pose a threat to the liberty of its citizens. Accordingly, the framers sought to minimize this threat by instituting a government that was to operate within confines established in a basic written document, the Constitution. As I noted in Chapter 1, it was to the courts that the task fell of policing the other branches of government in order to assure they stayed within the boundaries of the fundamental law. But, advocates of this perspective note, if the Supreme Court is to carry out its function of containing the other branches without itself operating as an illegitimate dictator, it must also operate within and be restrained by the Constitution.[3] If the Court, in policing the boundaries of the other branches of government, were not enforcing a body of law independent of the subjective will of the justices, the Court itself would be illegitimate. How, after all, in a democracy can a nonelected Court be justified, unless it functions as the implementer of a body of law (i.e., the Constitution, which itself was democratically adopted)?

The legitimacy of judicial review thus depends on the Constitution serving as an effective restraint on the justices. And if the Constitution is too plastic, too open to being used to legitimate current political fashion, it would have no more power to restrain than a rope of sand. We would lose both the possibility of a government under law, and the legitimacy of the institution of judicial review. Putting the Constitution into written form was meant to establish an explicit and permanent set of powers, rights and duties. As Justice Joseph Story wrote in his *Commentaries*, the Constitution "is to have a fixed, uniform, permanent construction. . . . The meaning of the constitution is fixed when it is adopted, and it is not different at any subsequent time when a court has occasion to pass upon it."[4]

---

[3] Perhaps the most accessible and powerful statement of originalism is to be found in Robert Bork, *The Tempting of America* (New York: The Free Press, 1990).

[4] Joseph Story, *Commentaries on the Constitution of the United States* (Boston: Hillard, Gray and Co., 1833), I, §426, p. 55.

Activist Originalism

Let's now look at one form of originalism, activist originalism. A clear example occurs in one of the most notorious cases in Supreme Court history, *Scott v. Sandford* (1857), in which the Court decided that Dred Scott, a slave, was not a "citizen" of the United States and, therefore, that he had no right to sue in federal courts. By barring his suit the Court prevented Scott from making the legal claim that he was no longer a slave because at one point in his life his master had taken him into free territory and that this had the legal effect of liberating him. Chief Justice Taney concluded, using historical references, that the framers never intended for blacks to be citizens of the United States, regardless of whether they became free or not. His approach to constitutional interpretation was an example of pure originalism.

> No one, we presume, supposes that any change in public opinion or feeling . . . should induce the Court to give the words of the Constitution a more liberal construction in their favor than they were intended to bear when the instrument was framed and adopted. Such an argument would be altogether inadmissible in any tribunal called on to interpret it. If any of its provisions are deemed unjust, there is a mode prescribed in the instrument itself by which it may be amended; but while it remains unaltered, it must be construed now as it was understood at the time of its adoption. It is not only the same words, but the same meaning. . . .

Originalism comfortably resides with judicial activism as evidenced by the work of Justice Sutherland. In the midst of the deep depression of the 1930s the Minnesota legislature adopted a law which extended the period for payment of mortgages and gave property owners a temporary respite against foreclosures for failure to meet mortgage payments (*Home Building & Loan Association v. Blaisdell* [1934]). When a home owner sought to take advantage of the provisions of the law, the Home Building & Loan Association argued that the law violated Article I, §10 of the Constitution which prohibited states from impairing the obligation of contracts. Despite the seemingly explicit language of the Constitution, a majority of the Court upheld the Minnesota law. Justice Sutherland, however, dissented. He offered this general approach to constitutional interpretation: "The whole aim of construction, as applied to a provision of the Constitution, is to discover the meaning, to ascertain and give effect to the intent, of its framers and the people who adopted it. . . . And if the meaning be at all doubtful, the doubt should be resolved, wherever reasonably possible to do so, in a way to forward the evident purpose with which the provision was adopted. . . ." Based on this approach to constitutional interpretation, he concluded that the contract clause was framed and adopted precisely to prevent debtors in times of emergency from using political power to obtain relief from their debts. He also observed that "A provision of the Constitution, it is hardly necessary to say, does not admit of two distinctly opposite interpretations. It does not mean one thing at one time and an entirely different thing at another time." Thus, the only question was whether the Minnesota law impaired the obligations of contract or not. "If it does not, the occasion to which it relates [the Depression] becomes immaterial. . . . If it does, the emergency no more furnishes a proper occasion for its exercise than if the emergency were non-existent." His final paragraph concluded with this classic statement of originalism: "If the provisions of the Constitution be not upheld when they pinch as well as when they comfort, they may as well be abandoned."

Until his retirement in January 1938, Justice Sutherland remained with Justices Van Deventer, Butler, and McReynolds foursquare against the reforms designed to cope with the Depression (e.g., regulation of farm prices, the devaluation of gold currency, regulations of hours and wages of workers, and the provision of unemployment compensation). Thus, originalism became associated with economic conservatism, but with the appointment of Justice Hugo Black to replace Van Deventer in 1937 it became evident that a consistent originalism could also end up supporting a portion of the liberal agenda.

Arguably Justice Hugo Black is the preeminent example of originalism coupled with activism. Justice Black approached his task with a deep-seated distrust of judicial power and the exercise of judicial choice. He saw in originalism a way to confine and restrain the Court. For much of his time on the Court a principal target of his criticism was the judicial philosophy espoused by a contemporary, Justice Felix Frankfurter, an advocate of noninterpretism coupled with restraint. (I shall return to Justice Frankfurter later.) Black expressed his approach by quoting this language from another case: "It is never to be forgotten that, in the construction of the language of the Constitution . . . as indeed in all other instances where construction becomes necessary, we are to place ourselves as nearly as possible in the condition of the men who framed the instrument" (*Adamson v. California* [1947]). Justice Black protested most vigorously against the reliance on materials external to the Constitution itself, such as the "community's sense of fair play and decency" and "traditions and conscience of our people." To invoke such materials, he argued, gave the Court "ultimate power over public policies in fields where no specific provision of the Constitution limits legislative power," and simultaneously threatened to "degrade the constitutional safeguards of the Bill of Rights."

Thus Justice Black sought in each case to base his conclusions on the text and the original intent of the framers. When the text was specific he would enforce it with uncompromising vigor. For example, Justice Black noted that "Some constitutional provisions are stated in absolute and unqualified language such, for illustration, as the First Amendment stating that no law shall be passed prohibiting the free exercise of religion or abridging the freedom of speech or press" (*Rochin v. California* [1952] [Black, J. concurring]). Given the absolutist language of the First Amendment, Justice Black dissented from a case upholding

Congress's authority to make criminal the advocacy of the violent overthrow of the government and the organizing of a group which advocates the overthrow and destruction of the government (*Dennis v. United States* [1951]). He wrote, "[I] cannot agree that the First Amendment permits us to sustain laws suppressing freedom of speech and press on the basis of Congress's or our own notions of mere 'reasonableness.' Such a doctrine waters down the First Amendment. . . . The Amendment so construed is not likely to protect any but those 'safe' or orthodox views which rarely need its protection."

Though Justice Black would provide absolute protection for free speech, he was careful to draw a distinction between "speech" and "conduct." Thus he would not have extended, as the Supreme Court has subsequently done, First Amendment protection to a person who burned an American flag, because flag-burning, despite the communicative intent of the protester, was conduct and not speech (*Street v. New York* [1969] [Black, J., dissenting]; *Texas v. Johnson* [1989]). But it was Justice Black who wrote the majority opinion in *Engle v. Vitale* (1962), the first Supreme Court case to strike down prayers in the public schools. Here again he found specific language in the Constitution to support his conclusion.

Despite his active protection of freedom of speech, religious freedom, and the rights of criminal defendants, Justice Black also used his approach with restraint. In *Katz v. United States* (1967) he dissented from the conclusion of the majority that the Fourth Amendment's prohibition against unreasonable searches extended to electronic eavesdropping on one end of a telephone conversation being conducted in a telephone booth. Justice Black, first, argued that the very phrasing of the amendment which protected "persons, houses, papers, and effects," connoted protection for tangible things; a conversation, he said, "under the normally accepted meanings of the words, can neither be searched nor seized." He moved then from the words of the text to the intent of the framers.

> Tapping telephone wires, of course, was an unknown possibility at the time the Fourth Amendment was adopted. But eavesdropping (and wiretapping is nothing more than eavesdropping by telephone) was . . . 'an ancient practice. . . .' There can be no doubt that the Framers were aware of this practice, and if they had desired to outlaw or restrict the use of evidence obtained by eavesdropping, I believe that they would have used the appropriate language to do so in the Fourth Amendment. They certainly would not have left such a task to the ingenuity of language-stretching judges . . . I will not distort the words of the Amendment in order to 'keep the Constitution up to date' or 'to bring it into harmony with the times.' It was never meant that this Court have such power, which in effect would make us a continuously functioning constitutional convention. (*Katz v. United States* [1967], pp. 366, 373)

The concluding paragraph of Justice Black's dissent in *Katz* struck a broader theme. "No general right is created by the [Fourth] Amendment so as to give this Court the unlimited power to hold unconstitutional everything which affects privacy." Here was a clear allusion to his dissent in another case in which the majority had concluded that "emanations" from the Fourth and other amendments created a general right of privacy, which included a right of married couples to use contraception (*Griswold v. Connecticut* [1965]). Justice Black said he found Connecticut's law barring the use of contraception as offensive as his brethren, and that, "I like my privacy as well as the next one, but I am nevertheless compelled to admit that government has a right to invade it unless prohibited by some specific constitutional [provision]."

But as consistent an originalist as Justice Black was, even he was not always consistent. To see this we need to compare his positions in two voting rights cases.

While a majority of the Court in *Harper v. Virginia State Board of Elections* (1966) struck down a poll tax (a $1.50 tax that had to be paid before voting in state elections) as discriminatory against the poor, Justice Black dissented. Again he accused the majority of reading into the Constitution its own preferred notions of what was good governmental policy. Neither the text of the Constitution nor history, he said, supported the majority's conclusion. But in *Baker v. Carr* (1962) and *Reynolds v. Sims* (1964) the Court went further in controlling the electoral systems of the states. It was in those reapportionment cases that the Court announced its famous one-person-one-vote formula and ordered that state legislatures create election districts that were roughly equal in population. Other advocates of originalism, for example, Justice Harlan, dissented, in opinions that could have been written by Justice Black. But in both these cases Justice Black voted with the majority. Lest it be thought that Justice Harlan was a more consistent originalist than Justice Black, it is worth noting that Justice Harlan concurred in *Griswold*, a case in which we just saw that Justice Black dissented.

Originalism and Restraint

In most people's mind originalism is probably more closely associated with judicial restraint and deference to the legislature. This is most clearly seen in the writings of Robert Bork whose nomination by President Reagan to the Supreme Court was defeated because of his views on constitutional interpretation. Bork argues that unless the evidence is clear—either from the text or evidence of the intent of the ratifers and framers—that the Constitution was to constrain the majority, the Court must not block the will of the majority as expressed in legislative action.[5] The silence of the Constitution does mean, he says, that we are at the mercy of the majority; this is precisely the meaning of majority rule.

Today, perhaps the most visible spokesperson on the Court for originalism is Chief Justice William Rehnquist. In Rehnquist's hands originalism is used to *broaden* government's authority to regulate speech. That is to say, the Chief

---

[5] Bork, *The Tempting of America*.

Justice would use the power of judicial review sparingly because he does not read the Constitution as imposing only certain narrowly defined limits on the other branches of government. For example, despite the seemingly absolute language of the First Amendment—Congress shall make *no* law abridging freedom of speech—Chief Justice Rehnquist has argued that the original intent of the framers did not mean to include, for example, speech proposing a commercial exchange, i.e., advertising (*Virginia Pharmacy Board v. Virginia Consumer Council* [1976]). Thus he would permit governmental regulation of commercial speech to the same extent government is otherwise permitted to regulate business. Similarly, he finds in the history of the First Amendment no special protection for "offensive," vulgar, and pornographic speech, the issuance of erroneous credit reports, nor any First Amendment right of newspapers to have access to criminal trials (*Board of Education v. Pico* [1982]; *Erznoznik v. City of Jacksonville* [1975]; *Richmond Newspapers Inc. v. Virginia* [1980]; *Dun & Bradstreet Inc. v. Greenmoss Builders Inc.* [1985]). Justice Black, in contrast, dissented from the conclusion of the majority that "obscenity is not expression protected by the First Amendment" (*Roth v. United States* [1957]). Even as to pure political speech, which Rehnquist acknowledges the framers did intend to protect, he has voted to support

- Restrictions of political signs near foreign embassies (*Boos v. Barry* [1988]),
- Restrictions on protests on public issues conducted near private homes (*Frisby v. Schultz* [1988]),
- The excluding of political advocacy organizations from inclusion in the Combined Federal Campaign, a collective charity drive aimed at federal employees (*Cornelius v. NAACP Legal Defense and Educational Fund, Inc.* [1985]),
- The firing of a clerical employee from a job in the county constable's office after she was overheard saying to a friend on the phone that she hoped next time someone attempted to assassinate President Reagan they would get him (*Rankin v. McPherson* [1987]).

From Justice Scalia, an advocate of originalism, we have gotten some extremely interesting comments upon the appropriate way to interpret tradition. The occasion for making these comments was a case that arose in California (*Michael H. v. Gerald D.* [1989]). Michael H. alleged that he had had an adulterous relationship with Carole D., and that he was the natural father of Victoria. Victoria now lived with Carole D. and Gerald D., husband and wife. Michael sought visitation and other rights with respect to Victoria. But California courts rejected his claims relying on the presumption established in California law that a child born to the wife is legitimately the child of that marriage. The California courts stuck to this presumption even though blood tests established a

98.07% probability that Michael H. was in fact the father. The California courts stated that the state law's presumption was really a "substantive rule of law" (i.e., the operative California law was that it favored preserving the family unit of husband and wife, that integrity of a family like that of Carole and Gerald not be impugned, and that somebody like Michael was not entitled to parental prerogatives, even if he was the natural father).

Michael claimed that he had a constitutional right as father to his relationship with Victoria and that California law violated his constitutional right. Such a constitutional right is not expressly mentioned in the Constitution; thus Scalia turned to tradition to determine whether "tradition" recognized Michael and Victoria as a family unit. His examination of tradition led him to the conclusion that historically this kind of relationship had not been treated as a family unit; hence Michael did not have a protected constitutional right. The California decision was upheld.

It was in this context that Scalia made his comments about the proper methodology for discovering and interpreting tradition. Scalia's approach was one of looking to tradition to see if, specifically, an *adulterous* natural father's parental prerogatives had historically been protected. Hence he examined our traditions by focusing on this narrow question, rather than on what tradition had to say about the prerogatives of "natural fathers" more generally, or of "parents." He supported his focusing on the specific question of what history had to say about parental prerogatives of adulterous natural fathers by arguing that he wanted to avoid, if possible, having to work with tradition broadly defined, e.g., rights of natural parents generally, "because general traditions provide such imprecise guidance. . . ." To have the justices, he argued, speculate about how general traditions apply to specific problems allows the justices "to dictate rather than discern society's own views. . . ." The problem with using tradition too broadly defined, he noted, was illustrated in this very case. He noted that *both* Justice O'Connor and Justice Brennan would have preferred to look at tradition in more broadly defined terms, yet each using a broader conception of tradition came to an opposite result, with O'Connor concurring in the Scalia judgment and Brennan dissenting. Hence, Scalia concluded that to look at tradition in a general and abstract way left "judges free to decide as they think best when the unanticipated occurs," but a "rule of law that binds neither by text nor by any particular identifiable tradition, is no rule of law at all" (*Michael H. v. Gerald D.* [1989]).

Justice Brennan attacked Scalia's methodology on several fronts. First, he charged that Scalia "pretends that tradition places a discernible border around the Constitution." Tradition cannot control judicial discretion, Brennan argued, because reasonable people can disagree (1) about the content of a particular tradition, (2) about which traditions are relevant, (3) about when a tradition is firm enough to be relied upon, and (4) about when it has become too obsolete to be relevant. Second, he argued that the particular way of using tradition—

looking at whether a specific variety of parenthood has been protected—had never before been used by the Court and was misguided. We ought to limit the role tradition plays in constitutional interpretation.

> In [Scalia's] constitutional universe, we may not take notice of the fact that the original reasons for the conclusive presumption of paternity are out of place in a world in which blood tests can prove virtually beyond a shadow of doubt who sired a particular child and in which the fact of illegitimacy no longer plays the burdensome and stigmatizing role it once did. [In] construing the Fourteenth Amendment to offer shelter only to those interests specifically protected by historical practice, moreover, the plurality ignores the kind of society in which our Constitution exists. . . . The document that the plurality construes today is unfamiliar to me. It is not the living charter that I have taken to be our Constitution; it is instead a stagnant, archaic, hidebound document steeped in the prejudices and superstitions of a time long past. (*Michael H. v. Gerald D.* [1989])

FORMS OF NONORIGINALISM

As illustrated by Brennan's remarks quoted in the previous paragraph, there are justices who advocate that the Constitution should be adaptable to new circumstances, to new problems, to new moral ideas. Many citizens believe with Chief Justice John Marshall that, unless the Constitution can adapt to the crises of human affairs, it cannot endure for ages (*McCulloch v. Maryland* [1819]). Hence, according to this view, both the legislatures and the Court should have the discretion to interpret the Constitution in ways that enable them to be responsive to changed circumstances without having to adjust the fundamental law through the cumbersome constitutional amendment process outlined in Article V. To accomplish this end, these advocates would permit opinion writers to reach outside the Constitution for materials to support their decisions. These justices believe they act legitimately when they turn, for example, to evidence of contemporary morality and readings of the text which take into account modern circumstances and modern technology.

Nonoriginalist Activists

Nonoriginalist activists have advanced both conservative and liberal causes. In the materials to follow most of the examples are from liberal nonoriginalist activists because it is their handiwork which has formed the basis of the current more conservative reaction.

Nonoriginalist Activists and Original Intent. Nonoriginalist activists have repeatedly said that the Constitution's meaning was not fixed as of its writing in 1789. Justice Douglas, in his opinion striking down the poll tax, wrote, ''In determining what lines are unconstitutionally discriminatory, we have never been confined to historic notions of equality any more than we have restricted due process to a fixed catalog of what was at a given time deemed to be the limits of fundamental rights. . . . Notions of what constitutes equal treatment for purposes of the Equal Protection Clause *do* change'' (*Harper v. Virginia State Board of Elections* [1966]). And Justice Brennan, in an opinion dissenting from the majority's decision to uphold the Nebraska legislature's practice of opening each day's session with a prayer led by a chaplain paid with public tax money, wrote,

> Finally, and most importantly, the argument tendered by the Court is misguided because the Constitution is not a static document whose meaning on every detail is fixed for all time by the life experience of the Framers. We have recognized in a wide variety of constitutional contexts that the practices that were in place at the time any particular guarantee was enacted into the Constitution do not necessarily fix forever the meaning of that guarantee. To be truly faithful to the Framers, ''our use of the history of their time must limit itself to broad purposes, not specific practices.'' (*Marsh v. Chambers* [1983])

In the case in which the Court upheld the Minnesota Mortgage Moratorium Law, despite the explicit language of the Constitution forbidding the impairment of contracts, Justice Hughes wrote that the notion that ''great clauses of the Constitution must be confined to the interpretation which the framers, with the conditions and outlook of their time, would have placed upon them . . . carries its own refutation'' (*Home Building & Loan Association v. Blaisdell* [1934]).

Liberal activists buttress their rejection of strict reliance on original intent with a corollary proposition. Justice Brennan expressed it best when he wrote, ''A too literal quest for the advice of the Founding Fathers . . . seems to me futile and misdirected'' (*Abington School District v. Schempp* [1963], [Brennan, J., concurring]). Hence, liberal nonoriginal activists tend to look at the intent of the framers and ratifiers as one of establishing broad principles, open to interpretation.

Nonoriginalist Activists and the Constitutional Text.   The activist nonoriginalist tends to use the text of the Constitution in characteristic ways.

- Interpreting the rights expressly mentioned in the constitutional text as serving broad and general *purposes*.
- Interpreting rights expressly mentioned in the constitutional text as having a broad *scope* (when a reasonable reading could result in giving the amendment a narrower scope). To give the text a broad reading extends its prohibitions to a wide range of governmental activities and, consequently, protects a wide range of private activities from governmental interference.
- Interpreting rights expressly mentioned in the constitutional text as providing support for *new rights* not expressly mentioned in the text.

A now notorious example of the first point can be found in the Supreme Court's decision in *Lochner v. New York* (1905). In that case a majority of activist nonoriginalist justices struck down a New York law which prohibited the employment of bakery employees for more than 10 hours a day or 60 hours a week. The Court ruled that the Fourteenth Amendment's due process clause (no state shall deprive any person of life, *liberty*, or property without due process of law) to mean that the term "liberty" included the notion of freedom of contract. The Court saw this law as an interference with the liberty of contract. In effect the Court concluded that the amendment protected the liberty to purchase and sell labor services regardless of the unequal bargaining position of employer and employee.

Let's take the example of the free speech clause of the First Amendment. The term "speech" could be narrowly confined to oral and printed expression. But nonorginalist justices say that the term "speech" extends to a wide range of "expressive activities." In *NAACP v. Button* (1963) Justice Brennan extended the protection of the free speech clause to the NAACP's activities in sponsoring litigation. (Justice Harlan's dissenting opinion argued that litigation was "conduct" and not "speech," therefore not an activity covered by the First Amendment.) To take another example, nonoriginalists on the Court have said that sleeping overnight in a park to demonstrate the plight of the homeless is a form of "speech." A majority of the Court refused to accept the truth of this proposition; the majority opinion written by Justice White merely said it would accept this proposition provisionally, only for the sake of argument. Justice White went on to uphold the National Park Service regulation prohibiting camping in certain parks even when done as part of political demonstration (*Clark v. Community for Creative Non-Violence* [1984]).

Arguably the most controversial step taken by nonoriginalist activists is the use of the constitutional text as a springboard for announcing new rights not expressly mentioned in the text. The techniques used to extrapolate these rights have been multiple.

- Justice Douglas said that the Third Amendment's prohibition against quartering soldiers, the Fourth Amendment's prohibition of unreasonable search and seizure, the Fifth Amendment's protection against self-incrimination, and the Ninth Amendment had "penumbras" formed by "emanations" which formed a general right of privacy which in turn included a right to use contraception (*Griswold v. Connecticut* [1965]).
- Justice Brennan wrote, "This Court has long ago recognized that the nature of our Federal union and our constitutional concepts of personal liberty unite to require that all citizens be free to travel throughout the length and breadth of our land uninhibited by statutes, rules, or regulations which unreasonably burden or restrict this movement. [W]e have no occasion to ascribe the source of this right to travel interstate to a

particular constitutional provision'' (*Shapiro v. Thompson* [1969]). Having recognized this right, Justice Brennan said the right was fundamental, and thus he used the strict scrutiny test to rule unconstitutional state laws denying welfare assistance to people who had not resided within the state for at least one year prior to applying for assistance.

- Justice Marshall argued in a dissenting opinion that education, which is not mentioned in the Constitution, was a ''fundamental interest'' to be vigorously protected by the Supreme Court. An adequate education was vital, he said, to the effective exercise of the right of freedom of speech and the vote, and thus there is an ''intimate relationship between a particular personal interest and specific constitutional guarantees,'' which warrants giving education ''special significance'' (*San Antonio Independent School District v. Rodriguez* [1973]).

- After examining the psychological pressures brought to bear upon people held in police custody for questioning, Chief Justice Warren wrote that ''In order to combat these pressures and to permit a full opportunity to exercise the privilege against self-incrimination, the accused must be adequately and effectively apprised of his rights and the exercise of those rights must be fully honored.'' Thus, in order to implement more effectively a right expressly mentioned in the Constitution (the Fifth Amendment's privilege against self-incrimination), the Chief Justice created a new right, the right to the ''Miranda warning.'' Arguing that new rights are needed as a way of instrumentally advancing and making more secure the broad purposes of expressly mentioned rights is a common nonoriginalist technique of justification (*Miranda v. Arizona* [1966]).

Using Implicit Premises. One of the most noted of the activist nonoriginalist decisions is *Baker v. Carr* (1962), which drastically modified the ''political question'' doctrine so as to make the federal courts available to review the apportionment of state legislatures. Prior decisions had held that the apportionment of state legislatures was a ''political question'' not appropriate for judicial action. In *Baker*, Justice Brennan's majority opinion reversed direction, thereby dramatically altering the relationship between the Supreme Court and the states. The nonoriginalist activists felt impelled to act because the state legislatures would themselves not act; those possessing disproportionate power in the legislatures simply had no incentive to give it up. Then, having decided that the ''political question'' doctrine did not in fact bar federal court review of state legislative apportionment, in *Reynolds v. Sims* (1964) the majority took the next step and struck down as unconstitutional the apportionment of the Alabama legislature. The opinion rested in part on a set of new principles Chief Justice Warren said were fundamental principles of representative government. Here are examples of the principles he found implicitly embedded in the Constitution:

Undoubtedly the right of suffrage is a fundamental matter in a free democratic society.

As long as ours is a representative form of government, [the] right to elect legislators in a free and unimpaired fashion is a bedrock of our political system.

Logically, in a society ostensibly grounded on representative government, it would seem reasonable that a majority of the people of a state could elect a majority of that State's legislators.

Since achieving of fair and effective representation for all citizens is concededly the basic aim of legislative apportionment, we conclude that [equal protection] guarantees the opportunity for equal participation by all voters in the election of state legislators.

Warren did not trace these principles back to a specific provision in the Constitution, nor to historical evidence of the framers' intent. The principles are simply discerned as logically necessary. Based on such general principles, the Chief Justice concluded that "the weight of a citizen's vote cannot be made to depend on where he lives," and, thus, a "State must make an honest and good faith effort to construct districts [which elect representatives to the legislature], in both houses of its legislature, as nearly of equal population as is practicable."

The dissenters rejected the fundamental principles Warren said were implicit in the Constitution. They viewed the majority opinion as nothing less than the imposition of the justice's own particular theory of democracy.

Drawing on New Materials. The extensive use of statistical data in constitutional debates began with Louis Brandeis. As an attorney in the earlier part of the century Brandeis gained fame for his arguments before the Court in support of liberal social legislation (e.g., regulations limiting the hours that an employer could require women to work). Brandeis' position was that as to this legislation the Court should act with restraint, that this legislation was "reasonable"; and he proved it by marshalling statistical evidence establishing the existence of a social problem the legislation was designed to address. Hence there came into existence the "Brandeis brief." These briefs were short on technical legal argument and long on statistical data elaborating on the social problem it was the purpose of the law to correct.

Though Brandeis used such data to *defend* liberal social legislation of government against the threat posed by a conservative activist court, in more recent years activists have used data and the analysis of social scientists to *attack* governmental policies. A sophisticated example of this practice can be found in a dissenting opinion by Justice Blackmun. His opinion uses complex social science studies to prove that the likelihood of a criminal defendant being given the death penalty dramatically changed depending on the race of the victim (i.e., the data showed that if one had killed a white person the chances of receiving the death penalty were significantly higher than if one had killed a black person). The less activist majority rejected the argument that this data demonstrated an equal protection violation (*McCleskey v. Kemp* [1987]).

Reliance on evidence of contemporary social values has characterized a number of the opinions written by nonoriginal activist justices. In *Furman v. Georgia* (1972) a majority of the Court, in a one-paragraph per curiam opinion, declared that the death penalty policy of the states in three cases was "cruel and unusual punishment" in violation of the Eighth Amendment. Three justices agreed with this conclusion, because the administration of capital punishment had been arbitrary and capricious, not because the penalty was unconstitutional per se. Justice Brennan went further in a concurring opinion. He took the position that the death penalty was never a permissible form of punishment. He argued, among other things, that the death penalty was contrary to contemporary community values. And to prove his point he used evidence of the infrequent use of the death penalty; he argued that this was an "objective indicator" that, despite public opinion polls showing support for the penalty, the penalty today was contrary to modern values.

In his concurring opinion Justice Marshall took a very different approach to the same question. He argued that "polling" data should be ignored because most people were not fully informed "as to the purposes of the penalty and its liabilities." He said that if people were to be presented with evidence on how, for example, the penalty is imposed in a discriminatory manner, and on the number of innocent people killed, he was convinced that "the average citizen would . . . find it shocking to his conscience and sense of justice. For this reason alone capital punishment cannot stand."

In addition to turning to new statistical data, activists have been willing to turn to a part of the Constitution other justices have refused to rely upon, the Ninth Amendment. ("The enumeration in the Constitution, of certain rights, shall not be construed to deny or disparage others retained by the people.") Until these activists came on the Court, this amendment had been referred to in passing in three cases. But, in the Connecticut contraception case, both the majority opinion and Justice Goldberg's concurring opinion resurrected the amendment to support the conclusion that there was a constitutional right to use contraception despite the fact such a right was not explicitly mentioned in the text of the Constitution itself. Today, a leading liberal scholar on constitutional law says that the Ninth Amendment "*at least* states a rule of construction pointing away from the reverse incorporation view that only the interests secured by the Bill of Rights are encompassed within the Fourteenth Amendment, and *at most* provides a positive source of law for fundamental but unmentioned rights.["6]

---

[6]Lawrence Tribe, *American Constitutional Law*, 2d ed. (Mineola, N.Y.: The Foundation Press, 1988), pp. 774–775.

Restraint and Nonoriginalism

Like the nonoriginalist activist, the nonoriginalist who acts with restraint acknowledges the open texture of constitutional language. Chief Justice Rehnquist has written that "The framers of the Constitution wisely spoke in general language and left to succeeding generations the task of applying that language to the unceasingly changing environment in which they would live. . . ."[7] These justices fully recognize the reality that they cannot avoid "making law," or "making policy." In other words, these justices have less faith that the mere words of the Constitution, or an analysis of original intent, can restrain the choices of the Court. However, they also believe that "making law and policy" is not a proper role of the Court, an unelected branch of government which cannot be held directly accountable to the ultimate sovereign, "the people." Accordingly, these justices proclaim that they must exercise their power of judicial review with restraint lest the tension between judicial review and democracy become intolerable. It is how these justices elaborate upon the theme of restraint that I shall look at here.

Let's begin with a brief look at Justice Oliver Wendell Holmes who said the following about the Constitution:

> [W]hen we are dealing with words that are also a constituent act, like the Constitution of the United States, we must realize that they have called into life a being the development of which could not have been foreseen completely by the most gifted of its begetters. It was enough for them to realize or to hope that they had created an organism; it has taken a century and cost their successors much sweat and blood to prove that they have created a nation. The case before us must be considered in light of our whole experience and not merely in that of what was said a hundred years ago. (*Missouri v. Holland* [1920])

Having recognized the possibilities of the growth of the Constitution, he was also careful to argue that the adaptation of the Constitution to changed circumstances was largely a matter to be left to the other branches of government. Thus, when a majority of the Court ruled unconstitutional, as an infringement of liberty, a law regulating the hours bakers could work, Justice Holmes dissented (*Lochner v. New York* [1905] [Holmes, J., dissenting]). For him the majority had simply imposed their preference for a laissez faire policy upon the country. He argued it was not the business of the Court to make value judgments on the social philosophy preferred by the legislature. "I think that the word liberty in the 14th Amendment is perverted when it is held to prevent the natural outcome of a dominant opinion, unless it can be said that a rational and fair man necessarily would admit that the statute proposed would infringe fundamental principles as they have been understood by the traditions of our people and our law." The Constitution, he said, "is not intended to embody a particular

---

[7] William H. Rehnquist, "The Notion of a Living Constitution," 54 *Tex. L. Rev.* 693, 694 (1976).

economic theory, whether of paternalism and the organic relation of the citizen to the State or of laissez faire.''

Though Justice Holmes generally advocated judicial respect for the constitutionality of the policies adopted by the other branches of government, when it came to freedom of speech, he was one of the most vocal proponents of strong judicial protection of free speech against legislative encroachment. It was Justice Holmes who, along with Justice Brandeis, developed the famous ''clear and present danger'' test. (See Chapter 1.) Unlike his agnosticism regarding economic theory, in this area he said the Constitution did embrace a particular theory of free speech. The Constitution, he said, embraced the concept of a free marketplace of ideas (*Abrams v. United States* [1919], [Holmes, J., dissenting]).

Thus, as Justice Holmes' judicial philosophy evolved, it carried within it an inconsistency. On the one hand, he believed in judicial restraint—a restraint which in the political climate in which he lived was ''supportive'' of the liberal social legislation being passed by the legislatures. On the other hand, he believed in strong judicial protection of freedom of speech.

Holmes never did explain why judicial restraint was appropriate when a legislature sought to regulate business, but that judicial activism was appropriate when legislatures regulated speech. Nor did he explain why the Constitution would embrace a theory of freedom of speech, but not a theory of economic relations. The intellectual effort to provide a rationale for this somewhat schizophrenic use of judicial power would only be made at a later date by other justices and commentators.

Justice Holmes left the Court in 1932, and seven years later another advocate of judicial restraint took a seat, Justice Felix Frankfurter. The inconsistency of Justice Holmes was not to be found in the opinions of Frankfurter. Frankfurter agreed with Justice Holmes' observation that ''The boundary at which the conflicting interests balance cannot be determined by any general formula in advance. . . .''[8] In Frankfurter's own words,[9]

> The answers that the Supreme Court is required to give are based on questions and on data that preclude automatic or even undoubting answers. If the materials on which judicial judgments must be based could be fed into a machine so as to produce ineluctable answers, if such were the nature of the problems that come before the Supreme Court and such were the answers expected, we could have IBM machines doing the work instead of judges.

He underscored this observation with the comment that ''Most constitutional issues derive from the broad standards of fairness written into the Constitution (e.g., 'due process,' 'equal protection of the laws,' 'just compensation'), and the

---

[8] Quoted in Felix Frankfurter, ''The Process of Judging in the Supreme Court,'' and reprinted in A. F. Westin, ed., *The Supreme Court: Views from Inside* (New York: W. W. Norton, 1961), p. 43.
[9] Ibid.

division of power as between the States and Nation. Such questions, by their very nature, allow a relatively wide play for individual legal judgment" (*United States v. Lovett* [1946]). He did add that there were certain clauses of the Constitution which had their source "in definite grievances and led the Fathers to proscribe against recurrence of their experience." As to these clauses, their meaning "was settled by history," which the judiciary had to respect.

Yet, while he stressed that the essence of his job was the exercise of judgment, Justice Frankfurter advocated the need for judicial restraint.

> It is not easy . . . to disregard one's own strongly held view of what is wise in the conduct of affairs. But it is not the business of this Court to pronounce policy. It must observe a fastidious regard for limitations on its own power, and this precludes the Court's giving effect to its own notions of what is wise or politic. That self-restraint is of the essence in the observance of the judicial oath, for the Constitution has not authorized the judges to sit in judgment on the wisdom of what Congress and the Executive Branch do. (*Trop v. Dulles* [1958], [Frankfurter, J., dissenting])

Thus, a central theme of Justice Frankfurter's opinions was deference to the judgment of the other branches of government. Let's return to the case discussed earlier in which the Court upheld criminal penalties for people who advocate the violent overthrow of the government (*Dennis v. United States* [1951]). Justice Black dissented from this conclusion, but Justice Frankfurter concurred. Characteristically, Frankfurter viewed the problem as one of balancing. In this case he saw that the balance to be struck was between the demands of free speech and the interest in national security. Striking that balance, he said, was beyond the capacity of the judiciary. And, he added, "Full responsibility for the choice cannot be given to the courts. Courts are not representative bodies." He was also concerned about the political vulnerability of the Court. "History teaches that the independence of the judiciary is jeopardized when courts become embroiled in the passions of the day and assume primary responsibility in choosing between competing political, economic and social pressures."

Note, it is common for advocates of judicial restraint to accord special weight to the interests asserted by the government in justification of its policy. It is, of course, easier to rule in favor of the government and uphold its policies when the reasons it offers for its policy are seen as especially significant.

But let's return to Justice Frankfurter. Despite the fact Justice Holmes was a model for him, Justice Frankfurter did not use his power vigorously to protect freedom of speech. He sought, as he said in his own words, "to avoid the mistake comparable to that made by those whom we criticized when dealing with the control of property."[10] In other words, he did not wish to make the mistake in

---

[10]Quoted in H. N. Hirsch, *The Enigma of Felix Frankfurter* (New York: Basic Books, 1981), p. 151.

the free speech cases that Justice Holmes said had been made by the Court in the economic regulation cases. Frankfurter rejected the proposition that there were certain preferred values in the Constitution, and he specifically rejected the idea that freedom of speech enjoyed a preferred position (*Kovacs v. Cooper* [1949], [Frankfurter, J., concurring]). This did not mean he did not on occasion vote against the government and in favor of freedom of speech, but he always did so after weighing and balancing the interests on both sides of the particular case (*Sweezy v. New Hampshire* [1957]).

Arguably, carried to extremes Justice Frankfurter's approach would have meant abdication by the Supreme Court of the power of judicial review. But, in fact, Frankfurter did not abdicate. In apparently striking contradiction to his preaching the doctrine of judicial self-restraint, he voted in certain criminal rights, religion, and academic freedom cases in favor of judicial control of the other branches of government. He reconciled this activism with his belief in restraint by saying that there were times when "the transgression of constitutional liberty is too plain for argument . . ." (*Minersville v. Gobitis* [1940]).

But simply declaring that a transgression is too plain to be debated is hardly a satisfactory basis by itself upon which to build a constitutional decision. To what materials did Justice Frankfurter turn in these cases? What could convince this justice that he had no choice in the matter? (This is an especially interesting question with regard to Frankfurter, since, if you recall, he premised his argument for judicial self-restraint on the assumption that, too often, the text of the Constitution did not provide the justices real guidance.) In other words, how could Frankfurter fulfill his ideal of disinterested judgment when he found the text of the Constitution too vague to provide external guidance?

Justice Frankfurter had to face up to this problem in *Rochin v. California* (1952). At issue in the case was whether the police had violated the "due process" clause of the Fourteenth Amendment when they used an emetic solution, forced into the suspected drug dealer's throat to make him throw up two capsules he had swallowed when he was arrested in his home. Writing for the majority, Justice Frankfurter concluded that the police had violated the due process clause. His opinion openly acknowledged that the clause was "vague," but he asserted that the Court could reach a decision with "detachment" and "objectivity," and that due process of law was not "a matter of judicial caprice." But, then, to justify his decision he resorted to personal subjective statements and vague references to "tradition" and the "conscience of our people." Thus, he wrote that "This is conduct that shocks the conscience. . . . They are methods too close to the rack and screw to permit of constitutional differentiation." To prevent this method of obtaining evidence was merely the application of a general principle, namely, it was only an instance "of the general requirement that States in their prosecutions respect certain decencies of civilized conduct." To sanction this mode of obtaining evidence, he said, "would be to afford brutality the cloak of law." In sum, this case of "stomach pumping'' offended "those canons of decency and fairness which express the notions of justice of English-speaking peoples. . . ."

Justice Black, who concurred in the judgment only, wrote that he would have resolved the case under the Fifth Amendment's prohibition against compelling a person to be a witness against himself. "[I] believe that faithful adherence to the specific guarantees in the Bill of Rights insures a more permanent protection of individual liberty than that which can be afforded by the nebulous standards stated by the majority." Then, in an attack on Frankfurter, he asked, "[W]hat avenues of investigation are open to discover 'canons' of conduct so universally favored that this Court should write them into the Constitution?'' He then expressed fear that the approach of the majority would return the Court to the days when it used its personal philosophy "to nullify state legislative programs passed to suppress evil economic practices."

The last Frankfurter opinion we shall look at is his concurring opinion in a case striking down, under the authority of the establishment clause, a program which allowed public school facilities to be used for religious instruction under an arrangement whereby religious teachers entered the public schools once a week to provide instruction to pupils who were released, with parental consent, from the regular school program (*McCollum v. Board of Education* [1948]). Justice Frankfurter began his opinion by asserting that the constitutional principle to be applied in the case was the principle requiring separation of church and state. He then acknowledged that formulation of the principle was only the beginning of the solution because "the meaning of a spacious conception like that of separation of Church and State" is only developed from case to case. Thus, once again his central problem was where to find a source which was external to his personal preferences as a basis for finding the meaning of this principle. His solution was similar to the one he hit upon in *Rochin*; Justice Frankfurter turned to history and tradition. His review of American history led him to the conclusion that the American community wanted a public education system that was wholly non-sectarian and secular. Then, looking at the facts of this case, he concluded that this released-time arrangement "presents powerful elements of inherent pressure by the school system in the interest of religious sects . . . The law of imitation operates, and non-conformity is not an outstanding characteristic of children. The result is an obvious pressure upon children to attend.'' Hence the principle of separation of church and state was violated.

By looking at history and tradition Justice Frankfurter hoped to find bases for decision external to his personal will. But Frankfurter's reading of American public education history is rather idiosyncratic, for, if anything stands out about that history, it is that public schools were, for the century in which they were in operation prior to the decision in *McCollum*, shot through and through with religion. It was the Protestant religious cast of these schools which led Catholics to depart from them and form their own private school system. Thus, as Justice Black observed, Frankfurter failed to find a basis for deciding which avoided the problem of "judicial caprice."

A Final Note on Originalism, Nonoriginalism, Activism, and Restraint

Since 1968 when Richard Nixon ran for the presidency the topics of activism and restraint, originalism and nonoriginalism have been at the center of national political debates. Nixon ran for the presidency promising to appoint people to the Court who would be "strict constructionists," and it was as President that Nixon had the opportunity to appoint Chief Justice Burger and Justices Blackmun, Powell, and Rehnquist. It was these appointments, combined especially with the appointments that President Reagan made of Rehnquist to the position of Chief Justice, and Justices O'Connor, Scalia, and Kennedy, that have moved the Court away from its nonoriginalist, activist, and liberal days of the Warren Court (1954–68).

In the midst of this significant change on the Court the justices and scholars have engaged in a long-running discussion of the pros and cons, and the justifications for activism versus restraint, originalism versus nonoriginalism. There is now an extensive literature on this topic with the originalist-restraint position best represented by Robert Bork's book, *The Tempting of America*, and the nonoriginalist-activist position represented best in the opinions, speeches, and articles of Justice William J. Brennan, e.g., "The Constitution of the United States."[11]

This debate raises fundamental questions about the meaning of the concept of the rule of law; constitutionalism; the legal and moral obligation of judges; the concepts of democracy, majority rule, and minority rights; and the role of the Supreme Court in our system of government. Any complete study of constitutional law and the American system of government must play close attention to this multi-layered and multi-sided debate.

CONCLUSION

Let's now link Chapter 3's discussion of strategies of justification with this chapter's discussion of the use of legal materials other than precedent. I noted in Chapter 3 that justices of all political persuasions can and have used deduction, balancing, or a mixture of these strategies. In contrast, when it comes to the use of legal materials, there is more of a pattern. Liberal justices generally do not place great stress on the importance of the framer's intent, whereas conservatives do. Thus a conservative might combine evidence of the intent of the framers with a strategy of deduction to arrive at conservative conclusions. For example, look at the dissenting opinion of Justice Sutherland in *Home Building & Loan*

---

[11] New York: The Free Press, 1990. Speech to the Text and Teaching Symposium, Georgetown University, Washington, D.C. (October, 12, 1985), reprinted in *The Great Debate: Interpreting Our Written Constitution* (Federalist Society, 1986), and in Sheldon Goldman and Austin Sarat, eds., *American Court Systems*, 2d ed. (New York: Longman, 1989).

Association v. Blaisdell (1934), discussed above at pp. 72–73. But while there is a clearer pattern here, one should also be aware that liberals are also capable of relying on original intent arguments, and a judicial conservative like Justice Frankfurter has combined evidence of contemporary values and a strategy of balancing to support conservative results. Justice Black read certain provisions of the Constitution almost literally and stressed the importance of original intent in opinions which reached judgments liberals could applaud. Thus, while one should be aware that today there is a loose correlation between political philosophy (liberalism and conservatism) and an attitude toward the use of legal materials, one should be aware that the correlation is not perfect.

Finally, as one moves toward the complete analysis of an opinion, one now should realize the necessity of taking into account both an opinion's strategy of justification, and the underlying philosophy of judicial review, i.e., whether the opinion reflects a version of originalism or nonoriginalism. The analysis cannot, however, stop here. One must also go on to consider the opinion's use of precedent, the topic of the next chapter.

THE OPINIONS OF CHIEF JUSTICE MARSHALL: AN ADDENDUM

In Chief Justice John Marshall, who was arguably the greatest justice to serve on the Court, we find embodied all the contradictions and tensions of American constitutional law. While he was a strong proponent of the rule of law and the Constitution as the fundamental and supreme law of the land, binding upon Congress and Court alike (*Marbury v. Madison* [1803]), he also recognized the need for adaptation and change:

> The subject is the execution of those great powers on which the welfare of the nation essentially depends. It must have been the intention of those who gave these powers to insure, as far as human prudence could insure, their beneficial execution. This could not be done by confining the choice of means to such narrow limits as not to leave it in the power of Congress to adopt any which might be appropriate, and which were conductive to the end. This provision is made in a constitution intended to endure for ages to come, and, consequently, to be adapted to the various *crises* of human affairs. . . . It would have been an unwise attempt to provide, by immutable rules, for exigencies which, if foreseen at all, must have been seen dimly, and which can be best provided for as they occur. . . . (*McCulloch v. Maryland* [1819])

In reliance on this philosophical attitude toward the Constitution, Chief Justice Marshall crafted his opinions using only a selected range of legal materials. Though Chief Justice Marshall made an occasional passing reference to the ''intent of the framers,'' he wrote his opinions primarily using other materials:

those abstract and general principles he found embodied in the Constitution; the specific text of the Constitution; and his desire that the Constitution be an effective and practical instrument (i.e., that it not be "a splendid bauble"). By relying on these materials Marshall's opinions, while dealing with some of the most contentious political issues of the day, did so in a way that seemed to elevate his opinions above the fray. Who could quarrel with decisions that seemed to flow so effortlessly from premises virtually no one could deny.

Let's now look a bit more closely at Chief Justice Marshall's use of these materials. After Congress chartered the Second Bank of the United States in 1816, the bank established branches in many states, including Maryland. In April 1818, the Maryland legislature adopted a law requiring all banks not chartered by the state (including the National Bank) to issue their notes only on stamped paper to be furnished by the state for a fee. The statute also provided for penalties for violators. A suit for violation of the statute was brought by Maryland against James McCulloch, Cashier of the Baltimore branch of the Bank of the United States. In effect, the suit demanded that the U.S. bank pay the state tax. There were two issues in the case: (a) Did Congress have the power to incorporate a national bank? and (b) Could Maryland, without violating the U.S. Constitution, tax the operations of the United States Bank?

Justice Marshall's handling of the second issue illustrates his method of working from general principles of the Constitution. He deployed several arguments to support the conclusion that Maryland's tax was unconstitutional, but the most central of his arguments, which used a strategy of deduction, can be restated as follows:

1. The Constitution declares that it and the laws made in pursuance thereof are the supreme law of the land. The people of the United States did not design their government to be dependent upon the states.
2. The power to tax is the power to destroy.
3. If Maryland's claim were to be upheld, this would change the character of the Constitution. The states would be capable of "arresting all the measures of the [federal] government, and of prostrating it at the foot of the states." Therefore, to uphold Maryland's claim would be to render empty and without meaning the declaration that the Constitution and the laws made in pursuance of it are the supreme law of the land.
4. Concluding, Chief Justice Marshall wrote that the judgment that the states have not the power to tax the operations of the federal government was an "unavoidable consequence of that supremacy which the constitution has declared."

Chief Justice Marshall's masterful use of general principles to reach specific conclusions is matched by his dexterity in working with specific words of the constitutional text. I return again to Marshall's opinion in the National Bank case and his response to Maryland's argument that Congress lacked the authority to incorporate the bank. Following the enumeration in Article I of Congress's power, an enumeration which makes no mention of authority to charter a bank, the Constitution states that Congress has the power "to make all laws which shall be necessary and proper for carrying into execution the foregoing powers. . . ." Maryland argued that this clause, despite appearances, was restrictive of the right of Congress to select the means for executing the enumerated powers. As Maryland read the term "necessary," it meant that Congress could pass laws only to execute the expressly granted powers which were "indispensable." In addressing this argument Chief Justice Marshall first observed that the term "necessary," as commonly used, is open to a variety of interpretations. He then added that "in its construction, the subject, the context, the intention of the person using them, are all to be taken into view. Let this be done in the case under consideration." There then followed a series of arguments to support a broad interpretation of the clause.

1. Considerations of prudence, he said, pointed to a broad interpretation. This argument is captured in the passage I quoted at length above in which Marshall notes that it "must have been" the intent of the framers to ensure beneficial execution of the power given to Congress.
2. A broad interpretation of the term was needed to sustain other laws passed by Congress. Congress has no express authority to punish those who rob the U.S. Mail, which it has explicit authority to establish. Hence, if Congress is to protect the mail system, we must abandon a limited construction of the word "necessary."
3. Only a broad interpretation of the word makes sense of the other key term used in the clause, the word "proper." Adding "proper" to the clause would be pointless if the legislature were already restricted to choosing only absolutely indispensable means.
4. A broad interpretation fits the intention of the constitutional convention. The narrow interpretation suggested by Maryland "would abridge, and almost annihilate this useful and necessary right of the legislature to select its means. That this could not be intended, is, . . . too apparent for controversy," for several reasons. The clause was "placed among the powers of Congress, not among the limitations on those powers." And its terms "purport to enlarge, not to diminish the power vested in the government."

The Chief Justice went on to admit that the powers of the government are limited and may not be transcended. He concluded this portion of the opinion by writing, "But we think the sound construction of the constitution must allow to the national legislature that discretion, with respect to the means by which the powers it confers are to be carried into execution, which will enable that body to perform the high duties assigned to it, in the manner most beneficial to the people. Let the end be legitimate, let it be within the scope of the constitution, and all the means which are appropriate, which are plainly adapted to that end, which are not prohibited, but consist with the letter and spirit of the constitution, are constitutional.''

I want at this point to compare the Chief Justice's work in the bank case with his very different approach in *Marbury v. Madison* (1803), the case in which the Court took for itself the power of judicial review. While in *McCulloch v. Maryland* (1819) the Chief Justice stressed that the Constitution was a practical document open to interpretation to meet human crises, in *Marbury* his language was very different. In *Marbury* he stressed that ours was a government whose powers were created and limited by ''the people.'' ''The powers of the legislature are defined and limited; and that those limits may not be mistaken, or forgotten, the constitution is written. To what purpose are powers limited, and to what purpose is that limitation committed to writing, if these limits may, at any time, be passed by those intended to be restrained?'' Based on this attitude Chief Justice Marshall in *Marbury* made no effort to explore provisions in the Constitution which could have been used to support a finding that Congress had the authority to adopt the law in question. In his drive to strike the law down, he makes no mention of the ''necessary and proper'' clause. Instead, all his attentions are focused on textual passages which he used to try to show that Congress lacked the authority to pass the law he and his colleagues declared unconstitutional.

These two opinions, one expanding Congress's authority and the other confining it, are both extraordinary pieces of judicial opinion writing. Chief Justice Marshall was adept at weaving together textual analysis, vague allusions to the intent of the framers, basic principles, and prudential considerations. His opinions seem both practical and logically unavoidable. He was a master of the judicial craft. Yet it also seems clear that he was capable of using his powers of persuasion to serve contradictory positions. In fact, one way to look at Chief Justice Marshall is that he had no consistent theory of constitutional interpretation, but only a clear political agenda which he brilliantly pursued. In *Marbury* his goals were to expand the power of the federal judiciary at the expense of Congress, while in *McCulloch* his goal was expansion of federal legislative power at the expense of the states. He achieved both these goals, but at the cost of pursuing a consistent approach to constitutional interpretation.

CHAPTER 5

Precedent

Precedent can be used in conjunction with all three of the basic strategies of justification, the analogy, deduction, and balancing. The interpretation and use of precedent is both a skill and an art in which the justices are very adept. This chapter will examine the basic techniques the justices use in working with precedent, an essential ingredient of most legal justifications.

A TERMINOLOGICAL INTERLUDE

There are a number of terms which frequently occur in constitutional law: (a) principles; (b) doctrines; (c) tests or standards of review; (d) rules; (e) the holding or the *ratio decidendi;* and (f) policy. Let's begin with the term "policy." Policy-making may be viewed as the process by which goals and the means to the goals are simultaneously considered and decided upon. Those who engage in policy-making may engage (are expected to?) in compromise and bargaining with a view to reaching mutually agreed upon solutions. In constitutional parlance, policy is something that only the legislature produces. Courts, it is frequently said, should not engage in policy-making. Courts, in theory, should only find, interpret, and apply the law.

Turning to "principles," "doctrines," "rules," "tests," and "standards of review," these terms are frequently used interchangeably. For example, the following formulation can be referred to as a principle, rule, doctrine, or test: Congress may regulate, pursuant to its authority to regulate interstate commerce, labor relations at even a "local" manufacturing plant, when it is part of an interstate manufacturing and sales company, because labor disruption at such a plant has "a most serious effect upon interstate commerce" *(National Labor Relations Board v. Jones & Laughlin Steel Corp.* [1937]). This might also be termed the "holding" or the *ratio decidendi* of *Jones & Laughlin.* This rule also provides a "test" for deciding future cases, namely, a regulation is permissible under the commerce clause if it regulates an activity which has a "substantial economic effect" upon interstate commerce.

But while terms like rule and principle are often used interchangeably, they can also be used with different meanings and implications. For example, the term "principle" sometimes means something very fundamental and enduring. Principles, in the grand sense of the word, tend to be cast in general *value-laden* terms that require further elaboration, and interpretation. For example, it might be said that the principle embodied in the equal protection clause of the Fourteenth Amendment is that all people should be treated with equal dignity and respect. But we also say that the Constitution embodies other "principles" which are less obviously moral statements (e.g., the principle of separation of powers).

Previous chapters spoke of "tests" or "standards of review." Recall that these are judicially created criteria that the Court says a governmental policy must satisfy in order to be constitutional. For example, a policy that treats different businesses differently is constitutional if "the classification is rationally related to a legitimate purpose." (This is the rational basis test used in equal protection cases.) Tests derive from or are based upon principles, which presumably are more fundamental and enduring.

"Rules" also derive from fundamental principles, and rules are typically formulated in more precise or narrow language than fundamental principles. For example, based in part on the principle of separation of powers the Supreme Court has developed certain rules (or doctrines) which it uses to guide its decisions whether or not to hear a case. One such rule is the rule that the Court will not render advisory opinions on questions submitted to them by a President seeking legal advice.

"The holding" of an opinion is (1) the material facts of the case, plus (2) the conclusion whether or not the government's policy is constitutional. (The holding can also be called the *ratio decidendi.*) For example, in *Zobel v. Williams* (1982) Alaska distributed its surplus tax revenues, derived from the taxation of its booming oil industry, to state residents in the form of a dividend which varied from resident to resident depending upon the length of time the resident had lived in the state after Alaska had become a state. The Court concluded that his policy violated the equal protection clause of the Fourteenth Amendment. Thus, "the holding in the case can be stated as follows: *It is a violation of the equal protection for a state to redistribute to residents of the state surplus tax revenues according to a formula which allocates the revenues proportionately in terms of the length of time the resident was in the state after it became a state.*

"The holding," *ratio decidendi,* rules, and principles of these opinions are not something to be "discovered," but something which is creatively formulated through an interpretation of the opinion. Take for example the formulation of the holding. As I indicated, the formulation of the holding requires a determination as to what are the "material" facts of the case. One says a fact was "material" to the decision if one is prepared to show that it was "necessary" or "sufficient" to the conclusion. If one is prepared to show that fact had a "causal" effect on the conclusion regarding constitutionality or unconstitutionality, then one is prepared to claim that fact was "material."

Back to *Zobel*—in reaching its decision the Court rejected Alaska's argument that the length of residency was a measure of a resident's contribution to the state, and, that the state could apportion the surplus funds in terms of a resident's contributions to the state. In other words, the Court also "held" (ruled, or concluded) that *rewarding citizens differentially for undefined past contributions of various kinds to the state is not a "legitimate state purpose."* Let me now suggest a yet more generalized version of "the holding": *It is a violation of the equal protection clause of the Fourteenth Amendment for a state to treat its bonafide law-abiding residents differently solely based on an assessment as to who is a more worthy citizen than another.*

To summarize, the terms principle, holding, rule, test, *ratio decidendi* are sometimes used interchangeably. Second, there are occasions when these words do not mean precisely the same thing. For example, "the holding" or *ratio decidendi* is often used in its technical meaning, namely, it is a rule-like statement formulated by combining (1) the *material* facts of the case with (2) the decision on whether the government's policy was constitutional or not.

Third, in justifying the "holding," or *ratio decidendi,* the Court will announce "principles," "rules," "tests," or "standards of review" which it then uses in justifying its holding. Hence, it is often said that the opinion "held" (ruled, or concluded) that in the future all problems of type X will be analyzed in terms of test H. These principles, rules, tests, and standards of review also carry precedential weight and are used by future courts in the justification of decisions they reach. These principles, rules, tests, and standards of review can in turn be used as part of a strategy of deduction; they may themselves be applied by further deduction, or may require balancing. In short, precedent can be used directly in an *analogical* argument, but in addition there are materials to be found in precedents that can be used in conjunction with deduction and balancing. Precedent has multiple uses.

The Court frequently uses "the holding" from a precedent in conjunction with an argument based on *analogy.* For example, using *Zobel* as an analogy one could argue that it would be unconstitutional for a state to apportion the size of a *tax exemption* in terms of the length of time a person resided in the state. Similarly, again by analogy, it arguably would be unconstitutional to give to longtime residents the opportunity to cast a vote worth five times the vote cast by a new arrival. Of course, one can always question whether the analogy is appropriate, and one might even ask whether my two conclusions are sound.

THE ENGLISH DOCTRINE OF PRECEDENT

The *Ratio Decidendi, Obiter Dictum,* and Distinguishing Cases

English common law courts express the justifications for their decisions by expressing reliance upon previous decisions. English courts do this in the name of the doctrine of precedent which says that two cases must be decided the same way if their "material" facts are the same.

Here is a simple example of the doctrine of precedent in operation. A case has come to court, let's call it case B, in which the defendant threatened to bring criminal charges against the plaintiff, a foreign servant-girl, if she did not provide certain information (*Janvier v. Sweeney* [1919]). The defendant's threat was an empty lie because he knew that any charges he might bring against the girl were baseless. Nevertheless, the girl became ill from the distress caused her by the threat. She sued the defendant. The court's opinion went roughly as follows:

> *Legal Premise:* Where the defendant has willfully told the plaintiff a lie that is likely to so frighten the plaintiff as to cause the plaintiff physical distress, the defendant is liable. (Premise based on precedent in prior case A.)
>
> *Factual Premise:* The defendant is this case told the plaintiff a lie that was likely, and did, in fact, so frighten the plaintiff as to cause the plaintiff physical distress. (Based on facts determined at the trial.)
>
> *Conclusion:* The defendant is liable.

Our concern is how the judge in case B went about developing his argument, and more specifically, how he went about establishing the legal premise which began his justification. He did this by following a four-step process.

Step One. First, judge B undertook a search for relevant precedent—precedent with material facts similar to the case before him. This search brought him to *Wilkinson v. Downton* (1897). The defendant in *Wilkinson*, as a practical joke, told the plaintiff that her husband had been seriously injured in an accident and had been sent with two broken legs to the Elms hospital at Leytonstone. This false statement so shocked the plaintiff that it produced vomiting, other serious physical consequences, and weeks of suffering. Previous to this "joke" she had not been in ill health nor had she ever exhibited any predisposition to nervous shock. The judge in *Wilkinson* (case A) noted that the defendant willfully did an act calculated to cause physical harm to the plaintiff, and that this was a proper legal basis on which to sue since there was no justification for the lie.

Step Two. Judge B recognized that the facts of case A were similar to, but not identical with, the facts of the case with the foreign servant-girl. Thus, his second step was to decide if the facts were similar enough in important respects that case

A should be treated as precedent for case B, or whether case A was *distinguishable* from case B. In fact he concluded that case A was *analogous* to case B; thus he decided not to *distinguish* case A, and used it to justify his decision in case B. (The judge in case B could have *distinguished* case A from B, and written an opinion saying prosecutors should be allowed to use threats of prosecution as a means of gathering information.)[1]

Step Three. The third step was to determine the *ratio decidendi* of the decision in case A. We know already that judge B interpreted the decision in case A to stand for the *ratio decidendi* stated above as the legal premise of the syllogism (Version 1). But how did judge B decide that this legal principle was the *ratio decidendi* of case A? The answer is that it took an act of *interpretation* to settle upon this particular version of the *ratio decidendi*. Here is another possible version of the *ratio decidendi* of case A.

> Where the defendant has willfully lied to the plaintiff by saying that a close family member has suffered a grievous injury and this lie causes such distress that the plaintiff suffers severe physical distress for a period of weeks, the defendant is liable. (Version 2)

This is a *narrower* version of the *ratio decidendi* because this rule would only cover cases in which the deliberate lie was about the well-being of a family member and the effect of the lie showed up as physical symptoms. If this were the "holding" of case A, then the court in case B would have a harder time using the precedent to justify a decision in favor of the servant-girl.

But, as we saw, judge B chose to interpret case A as establishing a more abstract and general *ratio decidendi*. Yet how did judge B conclude that the more general *ratio decidendi* was the better interpretation? And, why did not judge B interpret case A to stand for an even more abstract or general rule, namely, that any false statement told to anybody which causes any degree of mental distress is a basis for liability (Version 3)?

In English practice interpreting a case and choosing among possible versions of the *ratio decidendi* are guided by an important rule: "Courts do not accord to their predecessors an unlimited power of laying down wide rules."[2] Based on this principle a British judge would reject version 3 as an unnecessarily broad description of the holding of case A.

---

[1] Suppose, however, that the only precedent the judge in case B could find was cases in which the plaintiff deliberately inflicted physical harm by hitting the defendant. These cases involving a "battery" are *distinguishable*. Hence, finding no case like case B, the judge would have two choices: He could conclude that the plaintiff could win her suit since there is no binding rule which he could use to write a justification in support of the plaintiff, or he could "extend" the battery cases, use them to justify a decision that essentially made "new law."

[2] Glanville Williams, *Learning the Law*, 11th ed. (London: Stevens and Sons, 1982), p. 75.

Turning to version 2, though it is a plausible candidate, judge B might conclude that the first version best fits what he understands precedent A to have said; that is to say, the judge might conclude that even lies *not* told about family members were deemed harmful and were said to be a basis for suit.

Before moving on to step four, I would like to interject a comment about the concept of *obiter dictum*, or just plain "dictum." Dictum takes several forms. It can be an "aside," a "remark by the way," on a point of law not necessarily involved in the case before the court. For example, judge A noted that the plaintiff also sued the defendant for "deceit" as well as for intentionally inflicting emotional harm. To prove deceit the law requires that the plaintiff establish that the defendant lied, that the defendant intended the plaintiff to act on the lie, that the defendant relied on the lie, and that in so acting the plaintiff was injured. But judge A noted that the injury to the plaintiff did not arise because she "acted" on the basis of what the defendant said. Her shock and physical distress were simply a spontaneous reaction to the lie. Thus, judge A hinted, without actually deciding, that a suit for deceit would fail. But he did note that the plaintiff had another basis upon which to collect damages for the harm done, namely, her claim for infliction of emotional suffering. Accordingly, judge A's comments on the claim for "deceit" were dictum, a statement about the law unnecessary to the actual decision in case A.

One also finds dictum in an opinion when a judge makes what appears to be a legal ruling but his comments are based on hypothetical facts, facts not proven in the case. For example, suppose that judge B had said that he would have ruled differently if the defendant had lied to the plaintiff to force her to provide information necessary to protect the national security. This "exception" to liability for deliberately causing emotional distress would not be law, would not be binding on future courts, because it was not an issue argued before the court and the pronouncement of such an exception would have been unnecessary to the actual decision before the court in case B.

Finally, we can identify as dictum a holding or rule which is phrased by the judge in a manner that is unnecessarily broad for the purposes of the case he or she is deciding. Version 3 of the holding of the case discussed above, for example, covers problems and issues not actually before the court in case A. That is to say, this formulation covers more situations than were actually litigated before the court; hence this version is broader than necessary to describe the case. Accordingly, a judge who announced this as the holding of her decision could be said to have announced mere dictum.

Step Four. The last step judge B took in writing the opinion was to *apply* the *ratio decidendi* of case A to the facts of case B. Thus judge B concluded that the lie told the foreign servant-girl was the sort of lie likely to cause emotional distress, and the distress felt by the foreign servant-girl was of magnitude sufficient to allow recovery of damages. As I indicated above, judge B did make such findings of "fact" as reflected in the second, or factual, premise of the syllogism.

The Theory of the Doctrine of Precedent

The doctrine of precedent requires that a judge determine the *ratio decidendi* of a precedent; by imposing this requirement on future courts the doctrine assumes that there really is a *ratio decidendi* to be "discovered." Stated differently, the doctrine of precedent presupposes that the legal meaning of a prior opinion is not simply a rule subjectively read into the precedent by the judge in case B. That is, the doctrine assumes that judge B is not wholly free to imaginatively develop any version of a *ratio decidendi* he may want.

The doctrine of precedent also assumes that future courts are bound by the *ratio decidendi*. That is, when the precedent is relevant, these future judges must follow the precedent, even if they personally do not like the decision to which they are driven. Regardless of personal ideology, like cases, as a matter of fairness and rationality, should be treated alike.

Additional considerations other than fairness and rationality also support adherence to the doctrine. The doctrine of precedent preserves the predictability and stability of the law, as well as improving the efficiency and speed of judicial decision-making, since it is easier and faster to reach decisions in cases based on preexisting rules than to invent new rules each time a dispute comes to court.

One should now be able to predict some of the effects of the doctrine of precedent. The doctrine of precedent tends to make the law change slowly, a step at a time, incrementally. It limits sudden changes of direction or new doctrines. And it points to a set of special criteria for the selection of judges. That is, those recruited to be judges should be people who could be dispassionate and fair in interpreting and applying precedent. Under this system a judge's personal ideology becomes a matter of lesser importance than in a system in which judges are expected to "make" law. Finally, one would expect to find in the opinions of the judges operating in this system extensive and careful analysis of precedent.

THE DOCTRINE OF PRECEDENT (STARE DECISIS) IN THE SUPREME COURT

The Legal Status of the Doctrine of Precedent

Let's begin with an obvious, but important, point. Because the Supreme Court is the *supreme* court, there is no higher court whose precedents it must follow. This also means that a nineteenth-century Supreme Court has no greater legal authority than a twentieth-century Court merely because it sat earlier in history.

Now let's turn to a more fundamental observation. The basic starting point of all constitutional justifications must be the Constitution itself. Thus, in a paraphrase of Chief Justice Marshall's opinion in *Marbury v. Madison* (1803) I can write,

> It is a proposition too plain to be contested that either the Constitution controls any Supreme Court act repugnant to it, or the Court may alter the Constitution by an ordinary judicial opinion. Between these alternatives there is no middle ground. But certainly those who framed the Constitution contemplated that as the fundamental law of the nation, an opinion of the Court repugnant to the Constitution is void.

Given these assumptions, it follows, as night does the day, that the Supreme Court cannot and should not be bound to follow a precedent which it has itself concluded is not a sound interpretation of the Constitution. Stated differently, the justices are in a sense duty-bound to *overrule* their own precedent if they conclude upon further reflection that a decision was wrong. "[I]n cases involving the Federal Constitution, where correction through legislative action is practically impossible, this Court has often overruled its earlier decisions. The Court bows to the lessons of experience and the force of better reasoning, recognizing that the process of trial and error, so fruitful in the physical sciences, is appropriate also in the judicial function" (*United States v. Scott* [1978], quoting from *Burnet v. Coronado Oil & Gas Co.* [1932] [Brandeis, J., dissenting]). Similarly, the Court has written that "In constitutional questions, where correction depends upon amendment and not upon legislative action, this Court throughout its history has freely exercised its power to reexamine the basis of its constitutional decisions" (*Smith v. Allwright* [1944]).

Yet the Court finds itself on the horns of a dilemma. To overrule precedent undermines the principles behind the doctrine of precedent: the principle of fairness, predictability, and stability in the law, and the rule of law itself. The Court acknowledged this problem when it wrote, "[A]rguments continue to be made, in these cases as well, that we erred in interpreting the Constitution. Nonetheless, the doctrine of stare decisis, while perhaps never entirely persuasive on a constitutional question, is a doctrine that demands respect in a society governed by the rule of law. We respect it today and reaffirm *Roe v. Wade* [1973]" (*City of Akron v. Akron Center for Reproductive Health, Inc.* [1983]). In a similar vein Justice Marshall wrote,

> [T]oday's decision is supported, though not compelled, by the important doctrine of *stare decisis*, the means by which to ensure that the law will not merely change erratically, but will develop in a principled and intelligent fashion. That doctrine permits society to presume that bedrock principles are founded in the law rather than in the proclivities of individuals, thereby contributes to the integrity of our constitutional system of government, both in appearance and in fact. . . . [E]very successful proponent of overruling precedent has borne the

heavy burden of persuading the Court that changes in society or in the law dictate that the values served by *stare decisis* yield in favor of a great objective. [Here] we have been offered no reason to believe that any such metamorphosis has rendered the [rule] of reversal outdated, ill-founded, unworkable, or otherwise legitimately vulnerable to serious reconsideration. (*Vasquez v. Hillery* [1986])

But note that these pronouncements are balanced by other statements which openly show disrespect for the doctrine of precedent. For example, after Justice Rehnquist saw his majority opinion in *National League of Cities v. Usery* (1976) overruled in a subsequent case, *Garcia v. San Antonio Metropolitan Transit Authority* (1985), he wrote that he was confident that, in time, his position on the issues would once again "command the support of a majority of this Court." And in recent decisions involving the establishment clause of the First Amendment several justices have continued to hammer at trying to get long-held doctrine dropped, reexamined, and redefined. Justice Rehnquist was again one of the most outspoken of these justices when he wrote, "The 'wall of separation' between church and state is a metaphor based on bad history, a metaphor which has proved useless as a guide to judging. It should be frankly and explicitly abandoned" (*Wallace v. Jaffree* [1985], Rehnquist, J., dissenting). And Justice O'Connor has openly called for reconsideration of the rules announced in the abortion case (*Akron v. Akron Center for Reproductive Health* [1983], [O'Connor, J., dissenting]). The Court's most recent pronouncement on the doctrine is to be found in *Webster v. Reproductive Health Services* (1989) in which the Court wrote,

Stare decisis is a cornerstone of our legal system, but it has less power in constitutional cases, where, save for constitutional amendments, this Court is the only body able to make needed changes. We have not refrained from reconsideration of a prior construction of the Constitution that has proved 'unsound in principle and unworkable in practice.'[3]

The Judicial Attitude: A Closer Look

Judicial pronouncements aside, if we look at the Court's behavior we can see that the doctrine of precedent has little real hold upon the justices. First there is the fact that the Court has so often and so quickly reversed direction and overruled

---

[3]The Court's attitude toward the doctrine of stare decisis is different regarding decisions interpreting a federal statute. The Court has written, "The burden borne by the party advocating the abandonment of an established precedent is greater where the Court is asked to overrule a point of statutory construction. Considerations of stare decisis have special force in the area of statutory interpretation, for here, unlike in the context of constitutional interpretation, the legislative power is implicated, and Congress remains free to alter what we have done" (*Patterson v. McLean Credit Union* [1989]). See also *Booth v. Maryland* (1987) and *Smith v. Allwright* (1944).

precedent. In 1932 Justice Brandeis noted 28 instances in which the Court had overruled or qualified constitutional decisions (*Burnett v. Coronado Oil & Gas Co.* [1932] [Brandeis, J., dissenting]). Professor Maltz writes that

> even Justice Brandeis would have no doubt been surprised at the lack of respect among succeeding justices for the doctrine of stare decisis. In the twelve-year period from 1937 to 1949, for example, the Court overruled earlier constitutional decisions in twenty-one cases [footnotes omitted]—nearly as many as in the 140 years preceding Coronado Oil & Gas. By 1959, the number of instances in which the Court had reversals involving constitutional issues had grown to sixty; in the two decades which followed, the Court overruled constitutional cases on no less than forty-seven occasions. It seems fair to say that if a majority of the Warren or Burger Court has considered a case wrongly decided, no constitutional precedent—new or old—has been safe.[4]

The meandering course of constitutional doctrine was no more vividly on display than in *Chimel v. California* (1969), an opinion dealing with the proper scope of a search incident to a lawful arrest. The Court in *Chimel* concluded that an arresting officer constitutionally may search, without a warrant, the area within the arrestee's immediate control in order to remove weapons the arrestee might try to use, or to seize evidence he might try to conceal or destroy. In justifying this conclusion the Court reviewed the relevant precedent. Its review identified five previous changes of doctrine (its decision in *Chimel* represented a sixth change), and at one point the Court said about these changes that precedents "were thrown to the winds. . . ."

The cavalier attitude of one justice toward precedent can be illustrated with the opinions of Justice William Douglas. Justice Douglas wrote the majority opinion in *Skinner v. Oklahoma* (1942), which struck down an Oklahoma statute which provided for the compulsory sterilization after the third conviction for a felony involving moral turpitude, but excluding such felonies as embezzlement. His opinion contained a long passage which made the claim that procreation was one of the basic civil rights of man—a claim he made without citation to a single precedent or any other source material. And in *Harper v. Virginia Board of Elections* (1966) Justice Douglas wrote the majority opinion striking down the poll tax, a small fee a voter had to pay before being allowed to vote. His opinion brushed past the two previous cases in which the Court had upheld the poll tax. He made no reference to the doctrine of precedent. Instead, after a cursory summary of a number of other opinions, he announced that the earlier poll tax cases were now overruled. His reason was simply stated: "Notions of what constitutes equal treatment for purposes of the Equal Protection clause *do* change."

---

[4]Earl M. Maltz, "Some Thoughts on the Death of Stare Decisis in Constitutional Law," *Wisconsin Law Review*, 1980: 467.

In short, it is the rare justice who consistently takes an existing precedent as settled law and follows it despite the fact it means he must adopt a conclusion with which he personally disagrees. (Justice Scalia has written "[I] would think it a violation of my oath to adhere to what I consider a plainly unjustified intrusion upon the democratic process in order that the Court might save face" (*Booth v. Maryland* [1987]). But from time to time such adherence to precedent does occur. For example, in *Board of Education v. Allen* (1968) the Court declared that a complex system for lending to Catholic school pupils secular textbooks for use in secular courses did not violate the establishment clause; that is, the Court concluded that loan of these books had neither the purpose nor primary effect of advancing religion. By 1976 a majority of the Court had become more wary of financial arrangements that might, even indirectly, aid religion. (I am shamelessly summarizing here a great deal of complex and confusing material.) Thus, in *Wolman v. Walter* (1977) the Court *struck down* as unconstitutional the loan to nonpublic school students of such instructional materials as wall maps; but in that same case the Court also, once again, upheld the loan of secular textbooks. Now note the peculiar result the Court reached in this case. The Court concluded that it would *uphold,* based on *Allen,* the textbook loan as a matter of *stare decisis;* yet the Court also refused to rely on *Allen* to guide its decision regarding the loan of maps and other equipment. Having decided to follow *Allen* as to the loan of textbooks, but having refused to follow it as to the loan of maps, one would have expected the Court to distinguish books from maps. But it did not. Hence the Court reached inconsistent results on problems that we must assume the Court saw as identical.

DISTINGUISHING, RESTRICTING, AND EXPANDING PRECEDENT

Overruling precedent is only one way for the Court to change direction. The more usual methods employed by the Court are different, less obvious and less dramatic. Let me classify these techniques into two general categories: *narrowing the implications* of a precedent and *broadening the implications* of a precedent. The narrow interpretation of precedent takes two forms: (a) *distinguishing* the precedent so as to limit its implications, and (b) interpreting the "holding" (i.e., *ratio decidendi*), rules, doctrines, principles, and tests of the precedent narrowly or *restrictively* so as to limit the implications of the holding. The broad interpretation of precedent also takes two forms: (c) *generalizing* or *abstracting* from the facts of the precedent so that it applies to a wide range of new cases, and/or (d) interpreting broadly the "holding" (i.e., *ratio decidendi*), rules, doctrines, principles, and tests of the precedent so as to expand the implications of the precedent.

	Precedent Striking Down a Governmental Policy	Precedent Upholding a Governmental Policy
The Narrow Interpretation of Precedent	I Narrowing the Area of Impermissible Actions	II Narrowing the Area of Permissible Actions
The Broad Interpretation of Precedent	III Broadening the Area of Impermissible Actions	IV Broadening the Area of Permissible Actions

Let's now relate, in the form of a matrix, the broad and narrow interpretation of precedent to different categories of precedent: (1) precedent which involved a judgment to strike down as unconstitutional a governmental policy, and (2) precedent which involved a judgment to uphold a governmental policy.

Much of the rest of this chapter will elaborate on the matrix above. For the moment, note that cells I and IV are in a sense two sides of the same coin. That is to say, narrowing the area of impermissible actions (by narrowly interpreting precedent which struck down a governmental policy) has similar practical effects to broadening the area of permissible actions (by interpreting broadly precedent which upheld a governmental policy). The same is true as regards cells I and III: narrowing the area of permissible action has the same practical effect as broadening the area of impermissible action.

The materials which follow illustrate the techniques the justices have used in interpreting precedent narrowly or broadly. These are techniques employed by both liberal and conservative justices. That is, justices, regardless of political preference, use these techniques to step around precedent they find embarrassing, and to bring to their aid precedent they think useful.

Cell I. The Narrow Interpretation of a Precedent Striking Down a Governmental Policy (Expanding the Area of Permissible Activities, or Narrowing the Area of Impermissible Activities)

A precedent which struck down a governmental policy limits the future discretion of government—state, federal, or local. For example, at one time the police, before questioning a person in custody, had the choice of either informing a suspect that he could remain silent or not providing him with such information. After the decision in *Miranda v. Arizona* (1966) the police no longer have that choice—they now must provide the suspect with the so-called Miranda warning if they wish to use against him any statement he makes. But now notice this: When a future Court *narrowly* interprets *Miranda*, the Court in effect keeps to a minimum the restraints it imposes upon the other branch of government. The narrow interpretation of a precedent which struck down a governmental policy tells us that the Supreme Court is not prepared to go further in restricting the other branch of government's discretion. For example, several years after its decision in *Miranda v. Arizona,* the Court said that statements made in the absence of the proper warning could be used to impeach the accused's credibility by showing that these statements contradicted the testimony he gave at trial (*Harris v. New York* [1971]). Thus today the original *Miranda* case has been narrowly interpreted only to prohibit using Miranda-less statements to prove the accused's guilt, but not to prohibit their use to attack the accused's credibility.

Both liberal and conservative justices have narrowly interpreted precedent which struck down a governmental policy. Of course, the conservatives *narrowly* interpret cases the liberals would interpret broadly, and the liberals *narrowly* interpret precedent the conservatives would interpret broadly. I will begin illustrating these observations with examples of a conservative justice (1) *distinguishing* precedent and (2) *restrictively* interpreting a *ratio decidendi.*

Wisconsin v. Constantineau (1971) involved a statute which provided that certain public officials could in writing forbid the sale or gift of alcoholic beverages to a person who drank excessively (as defined in the law). The chief of police of Hartford without any notice or hearing posted a notice in liquor stores that Constantineau was not to be sold any liquor. Justice Douglas found that this "posting" was degrading, and he concluded it was unconstitutional. He wrote, "Where a person's good name, reputation, honor, or integrity is at stake because of what the government is doing to him, notice and an opportunity to be heard are essential." Thus, the Court seemed to say that before government could publicly brand someone with a stigmatizing label, they had to be provided with a hearing, an opportunity to defend their good name, and a chance to prevent the "posting."

The next case to arise was *Paul v. Davis* (1976) in which the chief of police of Louisville, Ky., distributed a flyer to merchants alerting them to active shoplifters, and Paul's name was on the list. (Paul had been charged with shoplifting but the case had been filed away and had never gone to trial.) Paul argued that the distribution of the flyer was unconstitutional under the ruling in *Wisconsin v. Constantineau.* Justice Rehnquist writing for the majority in *Davis* said the Wisconsin case should be read *narrowly.* Thus, Justice Rehnquist declared that the Wisconsin case involved two *material* facts: (a) the stigma imposed on Constantineau, and (b) the fact he was also denied the opportunity to buy liquor. Thus Justice Rehnquist concluded that it was not the stigma, standing alone, which Constantineau suffered which led to the declaration of unconstitutionality; also necessary to the declaration of unconstitutionality was his loss of the right to buy liquor. In other words, Justice Rehnquist concluded that the loss of the right to buy liquor was a *material* fact in the Wisconsin case. The Wisconsin case, he said, stood for the following *ratio decidendi:* The right to a hearing is only invokable when the stigma government has imposed is accompanied by a loss of some more tangible interest such as employment or a right a person previously had (e.g., the right to buy liquor). He thus *distinguished* the shoplifting case from the Wisconsin case on the ground that Davis had only been stigmatized and that alone was not sufficient to trigger a right to a hearing. Rehnquist "limited" the Wisconsin case to its set of facts (i.e., interpreted narrowly, and thus kept the restraints on government to a minimum).

The dissenting opinion of liberal Justice Brennan said the majority had "discredited the clear thrust" of the Wisconsin case and expressed the belief that "Today's decision must surely be a short-lived aberration." (More about the liberal response below.)

Let's now look at an example of a Chief Justice complaining that an opinion he wrote was being misinterpreted in a subsequent case. In *Richmond Newspapers, Inc. v. Virginia* (1980) Chief Justice Burger, in an opinion only announcing the judgment of a fragmented majority, concluded that the First Amendment did create a right on the part of the press to attend criminal trials. In an opinion that left the scope of that right of access in some doubt, the Chief Justice did suggest that there were occasions when criminal trials could be closed to the press. A trial judge, he wrote, could impose "reasonable limitations on access to a trial" in the interests of the fair administration of justice. Yet in striking down the closing of the trial in this case he said that "[a]bsent an overriding interest articulated in findings, the trial of a criminal cause must be open to the public."

The next case which brought into sharp focus the question of the precise meaning of the *Richmond Newspapers* case arose in Massachusetts where a state statute required the exclusion of the press and general public from the courtroom during the testimony of a minor who had allegedly been the victim of a sex offense (*Globe Newpaper Co. v. Superior Court* [1982]). The majority opinion of Justice Brennan *broadly* interpreted the *Richmond Newspapers* case and struck the statute down as a violation of the press's rights. Chief Justice Burger, who believed the Massachusetts law should have been upheld, dissented saying he disagreed with the majority's "expansive interpretation" of *Richmond Newspapers*. The precise point in dispute was the majority's reading the rule of *Richmond Newspapers* to require a showing of a compelling state interest before a trial could be closed (a showing they said was *not* made in this case). Chief Justice Burger interpreted the rule of *Richmond Newspapers* more *restrictively*. He said the rule in the precedent called only for a reasonable showing by the state, and that a reasonable showing (protecting minors from embarrassment) had been made here. The Chief Justice's *restrictive* reading of *Richmond Newspapers'* "rule" (test, or standard of review) would, thus, have allowed government more discretion in the closing of certain criminal trials.

Reducing the precedential value of doctrine by declaring it to be *obiter dictum* is another way of narrowly interpreting a precedent. The precedent given this treatment by liberal justices was *Pennsylvania Coal Co. v. Mahon* (1922).

The case involved a Pennsylvania statute that prohibited the mining of coal in such a way as to cause the subsidence of, among other things, people's homes. The plaintiff in the case sought enforcement of the law against the coal company in order to protect his house from subsiding because of the coal mining under it. The coal company claimed that to enforce the law against it would be a "taking" of its property (the coal company had a deed giving it the right to remove all coal even if it hurt the surface structures) without just compensation in violation of the Fifth Amendment. The Supreme Court agreed.

Many years later the Court faced the question of what precisely was the *Mahon* holding. Here are two possible versions of the *ratio decidendi* of *Mahon:*

A. A regulatory law which goes "too far" in limiting the use by a property owner (the coal company) of its property is a "taking" even if it serves a public purpose. (The opinion in *Mahon* actually stated this rule. To accept this rule as the holding could severely restrain government and improve the protection of private property against governmental control, depending on how the phrase "too far" were interpreted.)

B. A law which limits the use of one's property merely to protect the interest of one other private individual (the homeowner in *Mahon*) does not serve a sufficient public interest, thus constitutes a "taking." (This version of the *ratio decidendi* sharply limits the implications of *Mahon*. That is to say, to read the case this way means government may engage in extensive regulations so long as it is not intended to help only one single private individual. This *narrow* version expands government's authority.)

In 1987 a liberal majority of the Court said it was version "B" which had been embraced in *Mahon* (*Keystone Coal Association v. DeBenedictis* [1987]). The liberals argued that it was only the narrow issue of the enforcement of the law to protect a single property owner which came up in *Mahon*. Hence the liberals in *DeBenedictis* said it was not necessary for the Court in *Mahon* to discuss the broader version of the *ratio decidendi* in order to decide the specific case before it. That is, *Mahon* involved only the enforcement of the law at the behest of a single homeowner. Thus, those passages in *Mahon* which took up the broader *ratio decidendi* were merely *advisory* and without precedential value.

Note, by saying that *Mahon* was limited to a narrow problem and a narrow *ratio decidendi*, the liberal majority in *DeBenedictis distinguished* the two cases. The Court in *DeBenedictis* said these restrictions were constitutional, were not a "taking" without compensation because, among other reasons, they served an important public purpose and were not merely directed to protecting the interest of a single property owner. This freed the liberal majority in *DeBenedictis* to reach a different conclusion in *DeBenedictis* from that reached in *Mahon*. In fact, the Court in *DeBenedictis* upheld another Pennsylvania statute which placed tough restrictions on coal mining for a variety of environmental reasons.

In sum, this section of the chapter has illustrated three ways of reading precedent narrowly: (1) elevating certain facts to the status of being material to the decision, and then distinguishing the precedent, (2) interpreting the rule of a precedent narrowly, and (3) determining that a particular rule was mere dictum.

Cell II. The Narrow Interpretation of Precedents Upholding a Governmental Policy (Limiting the Area of Permissible Action)

A justice who finds that a particular precedent upholding a governmental policy expands governmental power in a way he or she disagrees with will seek to limit that precedent. A standard technique for doing this is to limit the meaning of the precedent to its precise facts. Consider the following example.

Of particular importance to liberal justices has been their effort to limit any precedent which seems to expand government's authority to promote or accommodate religion. For example, some years ago the Court upheld the "released time" arrangement whereby students who wished to engage in religious study were released from school an hour early to permit them to attend religious centers for religious study and devotional exercises. The remaining students stayed in the classrooms (*Zorach v. Clausen* [1952]). In the second case the Court upheld New York's policy of exempting from property tax liability a broad classification of charitable organizations including church and religious property (*Walz v. Tax Commission* [1970]). In the years following the issuance of these decisions, liberal justices have worked mightily to assure that the authoritative interpretation of these opinions narrows their scope. Justice Brennan, for example, has characterized *Zorach* in the following terms: The released time program in that case merely lifted a "substantial burden" (the legal obligation to attend the public school) on the free exercise of religion while not imposing any costs on the other students or their parents who did not participate in the program. In reading *Zorach* this way he seeks to sharply limit the occasions on which government can accommodate religious interests. As for *Walz*, Justice Brennan has taken the position that *material* to the decision in that case was the fact that it extended to a whole class of charitable property and was not limited to, nor did it single out for special treatment, religious property.

In a subsequent case Justice Brennan used these narrow readings of *Zorach* in his majority opinion striking down a Texas law exempting religious periodicals from the state sales tax (*Texas Monthly, Inc. v. Bullock* [1989]). He noted, among other things, that the Texas law exempted *only* religious publications, that the sales tax imposed no substantial burden on the free exercise of religion, and that the exemption could impose a burden on nonbeneficiaries of the exemption by forcing all other taxpayers to become indirect and vicarious donors to the religious organizations.

The conservative dissenters in *Bullock,* of course, objected to the majority's interpretation of the precedent. Justice Scalia specifically attacked Brennan's interpretation of *Walz.* Without going into the details of his argument, let me just note that Scalia insisted that there was evidence in the text of the *Walz* opinion itself, and other materials, establishing that the basic thrust of the exemption approved of in *Walz* had been directed toward specifically exempting religious organizations. He thus saw no distinction between *Walz* and the facts of *Bullock.* In his view precedent and the Constitution authorized government to exempt religious organizations, within bounds that he did not delineate, from legal burdens in order to reduce governmental interference with the exercise of religion.

Cell III. The Broad Interpretation of Precedent Striking Down a Governmental Policy (Expanding the Area of Unconstitutionality)

The broad interpretation of a precedent which struck down a governmental policy has the effect of further restricting government's discretion. With this understanding one should not be surprised to learn that liberals broadly interpreted precedent which blocked governmental policies which interfered with civil rights, civil liberties, and the rights of the criminally accused. Recall the Wisconsin case involving the posting of lists of people who drank to excess and Justice Rehnquist's narrow interpretation of the case in which he stressed as *material* the loss of the right to purchase liquor. Now let's look at Justice Brennan's interpretation of the liquor case as he outlined it in the subsequent shoplifting case (*Paul v. Davis* [1976]). He attacked Rehnquist's narrow interpretation of the liquor case on two grounds. First, Brennan quoted passages from the Wisconsin opinion which seemed to indicate that the Court had been solely concerned with the stigmatizing effect of the posted list, and not the loss of the right to buy liquor: " 'The *only* issue present here is whether the label . . . is such a stigma . . . that procedural due process requires notice and an opportunity to be heard.' " Second, he said the reference in the Wisconsin opinion to the loss of liquor-buying rights was only there as part of a complete presentation of the facts and "nowise implied any limitation upon the application of the principles announced." In short, for Brennan the loss of the right to buy liquor in the Wisconsin case was *not* a *material* fact and not a basis upon which to *distinguish* it from the shoplifting case.

That is to say, Justice Brennan used the Wisconsin case as an analogy for deciding *Paul v. Davis.* He did this by abstracting and generalizing from the facts of the Wisconsin case, by downplaying some of the particularities of the Wisconsin case, and, thereby, making it more generally applicable.

Here is another technique justices use for broadly interpreting a precedent.

In *Weeks v. United States* (1914) the Supreme Court announced the "exclusionary rule"—the rule holds that evidence illegally seized by the police from the accused in violation of the Fourth Amendment may not be used in trial to prove the guilt of the accused. Many years after the announcement of this rule the Court dealt with two issues regarding the scope of the rule: first, whether the exclusionary rule could be invoked to block introduction of evidence to a grand jury (as opposed to a criminal trial), and, second, whether the exclusionary rule applied to evidence seized by the police based on a search warrant issued by a magistrate—a search warrant which itself ultimately proved to be invalid but which the police relied upon in good faith (*United States v. Calandra* [1974]; *United States v. Leon* [1984]). The liberals, who were in the minority in both cases, answered both questions "yes" by *broadly* interpreting *Weeks.* Though *Weeks* did not involve the precise issues involved in *Calandra* and *Leon,* the liberals said *Weeks controlled* in both cases. The strategy the liberals followed in giving *Weeks* a broad interpretation involved several steps.

1. They interpreted *Weeks* as having based the exclusionary rule on two goals: the goal to protect the integrity of the *judicial* system by not permitting it to use illegally seized evidence, and the goal of deterring the *police* by not letting them profit from their lawless behavior.
2. The liberals also said *Weeks* recognized that the Fourth Amendment privacy right was a personal constitutional right which included the right of the accused to exclude all illegally seized evidence.

Thus the liberals rejected the conservatives' interpretation of *Weeks.* As the conservatives read *Weeks,* the exclusionary rule's purpose was solely to deter the *police,* not to redress an injury to the privacy of the search victim. The exclusionary rule, said the conservatives, was a *remedy* not a *right,* and the application of remedies in a particular situation depends on calculating the costs and benefits of using it. In both *Calandra* and *Leon* a conservative majority concluded that the costs of applying the exclusionary rule outweighed the benefits; hence illegally seized evidence may today be used in a grand jury proceeding and may be used in a criminal trial if the police acted in good faith on a warrant.

But let's return to the liberals' method for interpreting *Weeks broadly.* Most important, they found in *Weeks* two rationales for the exclusionary rule. The rule, they said, had to be understood in light of both these goals as well as the fact it was a personal constitutional right of the accused. The twin goals of the rule, and its status as a personal right, made the rule applicable to every aspect of the criminal justice system. In short, the liberals broadened the application of the rule by viewing the rule as serving very broad goals and purposes. Interpreting a rule in this way is a classic method of assuring its broad application. In this instance the broad reading of the rule would have restricted the area of permissible governmental action (i.e., would have made more governmental policies unconstitutional).

Cell IV. The Broad Interpretation of Precedent Upholding a Governmental Policy (Expanding the Area of Permissible Action)

Liberals and conservatives on the Court have been engaged in a long struggle over the interpretation of the establishment clause of the First Amendment and, specifically, the issue of how much and what kind of governmental assistance may flow to religious organizations. While the liberals have tried to block most forms of assistance, the conservatives have tried to adjust the spigot to a more open position.

In 1988 the liberals and conservatives once again clashed over the constitutionality of providing financial funds to various organizations, including religious organizations, for services and research related to teenage sexuality (*Bowen v. Kendrick* [1988]). Under the law authorizing the grants, religious organizations which received funds were not restricted from, for example, providing counseling on sexual matters from a religious perspective. The federal program was challenged on the grounds that the grant money would be used by religious organizations to promote their religiously based views on abortion, contraception, and related sexual topics. Chief Justice Rehnquist wrote the majority opinion which upheld the law as written ("on its face") without reaching the question whether the law as implemented ("as applied") was constitutional. I will not explore all the aspects of Rehnquist's opinion, but will instead concentrate on his interpretation of one precedent which he used to support his conclusion that the funding program was constitutional.

Almost twenty years prior to the *Bowen* case the Court upheld the provision of financial aid to colleges, including religious colleges, to assist in the construction of new facilities which could be used only for secular purposes (*Tilton v. Richardson* [1971]). (Incidentally, this decision stands in marked contrast to the Court's basic resistance to providing financial assistance to religiously-affiliated elementary and secondary schools. I will not discuss these seemingly inconsistent results.) Chief Justice Rehnquist in *Bowen* interpreted *Tilton* as standing for the following propositions: (a) A general grant program may be established even if it is foreseeable that some proposition of the recipients would be religiously affiliated and pervasively sectarian; (b) Prior cases do not warrant creating the presumption that pervasively religious institutions are not capable of using federal funds in a secular manner.

Now let's look at how Chief Justice Rehnquist arrived at these propositions. To interpret *Tilton* in this way Rehnquist had to *ignore* the following facts and comments found in the *Tilton* opinion. That is, he overlooked them, and thus implicitly concluded that the following matters were *not material* to the decision in *Tilton*.

- The law which was upheld in *Tilton* specifically forbade using the federal funds to build buildings to be used for sectarian purposes.
- Religious indoctrination was not a substantial purpose or activity of the church-related colleges; hence it was not likely that religion would permeate the area of secular education.
- Colleges and universities stress the importance of academic freedom and free and critical responses from the students.
- The students served by colleges and universities were not impressionable, hence less susceptible to religious indoctrination.

If we take these comments of the *Tilton* Court into account, the *ratio decidendi* of the opinion is much narrower than as described by Chief Justice Rehnquist. For example, the more accurate formulation would look something like this. Financial assistance to religiously affiliated organizations is permissible *only if* the aid is limited to assisting secular activities and there is reason to believe, given the nature of the organizations assisted, that they do not have as a substantial purpose religious indoctrination and their clients are not expected or are likely passively to accept religious indoctrination. Clearly, if this were the *ratio decidendi* of *Tilton*, then the aid program in *Bowen* would be unconstitutional. But, by giving *Tilton* a different interpretation, Rehnquist could use it to support his conclusion upholding the *Bowen* grant program. The liberals on the Court in their dissenting opinion obviously took a narrower view of *Tilton*.

Stated somewhat differently, Rehnquist chose to use precedent as a relevant *analogy* by ignoring certain facts of the precedent. He *generalized* and *abstracted* from the precedent in building his argument for upholding governmental authority. The liberals, on the other hand, chose to emphasize those facts in *Tilton* which Rehnquist chose to ignore.

CONCLUDING OBSERVATIONS

Our discussion has illustrated the following techniques for interpreting precedent: distinguishing precedent; determining the *ratio decidendi* strictly in light of the facts of the case (i.e., counting as material all the facts of the case); eliminating as not material to the decision and formulation of the *ratio decidendi* certain facts of the precedent; generalizing and abstracting from the specific facts of a case; arguing by analogy; the restrictive reading of a rule or test announced in the case; the broad reading of a rule announced in a case; determining that what appears to be either the *ratio decidendi* or rule is in fact *obiter dictum*.

It is common for a justice to employ all these techniques in building a justification. When you read an opinion you will see the opinion writer distinguish away the precedent he or she wants to avoid. You will see the justice seeking to declare as *obiter dicta* other comments made in an opinion he or she wishes to dispose of. You will then see the writer accept other precedent as relevant, and then by use of an analogy support his or her decision. Yet other precedent will be interpreted to determine its rules, tests, or its *ratio decidendi*. These rules, tests, and *ratio decidendi* may themselves undergo further interpretation—either a broad or narrow construction. The writer will then apply these rules and tests to the facts of the case in order to justify the decision.

By now it should be clear that precedent is a fairly plastic substance that can be used in a variety of ways to support and challenge a variety of positions. I am not saying that precedent is infinitely plastic, but certainly it is hard to say that there is a single correct interpretation of a precedent. Precedent is available to be used by both the majority and dissenting justices in ways they think best supports their position. Thus, you should be wary when a justice announces with great certitude that precedent A means X. You can be sure that there may be yet other plausible versions of the precedent, and more often than not the dissent will bring at least some of these alternative interpretations to your attention.

These last points are illustrated by the treatment of the Court of a single case. As conservative majorities have succeeded liberal majorities, or liberal majorities succeeded conservative majorities, these changing majorities have handled precedent as if it were an accordion. Thus we see a given precedent being expanded and contracted as different majorities take control of the Court.

Take, for example, *Pierce v. Society of Sisters* (1925), a case in which a conservative majority struck down under the Fourteenth Amendment a law which would have required all children to attend only public schools, not private schools. The case was brought by a private religious school and a private military academy; hence one plausible reading of the opinion is that the Court struck down the state's policy because it interfered with the right of these private schools to engage in business. The case was, in fact, decided at a time when the Court was hostile toward governmental regulation of business. In another case, also involving the regulation of private schools, Justice Holmes commented on this hostility in a dissent in which he stressed the importance of judicial restraint and the importance of allowing the legislature to experiment with economic regulation (*Bartels v. Iowa* [1923] [Holmes, J., dissenting]).

While *Pierce* can be read as a business regulation case, it also lends itself to broader interpretations. For example, in the contraception case, *Griswold v. Connecticut* (1965), a liberal court broadly described *Pierce* as standing for the proposition that the right of freedom of speech includes ''the right to distribute, the right to receive, the right to read [and] freedom of inquiry, freedom of thought, and freedom to [teach].'' But in 1972 *Pierce* was narrowed to merely protect the traditional interests of parents with respect to the religious upbringing of their children (*Wisconsin v. Yoder* [1972]). Then in the abortion decision, *Roe v. Wade* (1973), the majority described *Pierce* somewhat more broadly when it said that it stood for the notion that the Constitution protects certain zones of privacy that extend to child-rearing and education. Later still, in *Moore v. East Cleveland* (1976) and *Santosky v. Kramer* (1982), the Court broadened *Pierce* further, describing it as standing for the principle that there is a private realm of family life the state cannot enter. *Pierce* again drastically expanded in meaning in 1984 when a majority of the Court used it to support the principle that "the formation and preservation of certain kinds of highly personal relationships" must be afforded "a substantial measure of sanctuary from unjustified interference by the State" *Roberts v. United States Jaycees* [1984]). By 1988 *Pierce* was once again contracted. In a case decided by a conservative majority the Court said that homosexuals had no constitutional right to engage in sodomy, and *Pierce* dealt with child-rearing and education (*Bowers v. Hardwick* [1986]).

Are any of these interpretations of *Pierce* "wrong"? Probably not in any absolute sense. Each reading is a reasonable or plausible interpretation of the opinion. Hence we are left with the following propositions:

- A given precedent is available to be used in a variety of ways to support a variety of propositions. Perhaps only the imagination of the justice limits the use to which a precedent may be put.
- The justices frequently cite precedent as standing for broad and general propositions which are, at best, only loosely related to the actual text of the precedent itself.
- There are few, if any, clear standards as to which interpretation is the single best, much less, the *only* acceptable interpretation.
- The authoritative specification of the meaning of a precedent can and does change over time as subsequent Courts interpret it.

CHAPTER 6

Understanding a
Supreme Court Opinion

In Chapters 3, 4, and 5 we examined the craft of judicial opinion writing by dividing the topic up into separate parts. Chapter 3 took up the topic of strategies of justification, specifically, the analogy, balancing, deduction, and combinations of balancing and deduction. Chapter 4 examined the use of text, original intent, tradition, the tacit postulates of the Constitution, and considerations of prudence in the writing of an opinion. Then in Chapter 5 we looked at the Supreme Court's use of precedent. Having pulled the opinion apart into its basic components, it is now time to recombine the elements. We'll do this by looking at the majority and dissenting opinions in one case, *Allied Structural Steel Co. v. Spannaus* (1978).

THE FACTS

Allied Structural Steel (Allied) maintained an office in Minnesota with 30 employees. Employees of Allied were covered by a company pension plan, but only employees who met certain requirements having to do with length of employment in the firm were "vested" in the plan. Employees who were not vested and who quit, or were discharged prior to age 65 did not acquire any pension rights. Allied was the only contributor to the pension trust fund, and the plan did not require the company to make any specific contributions nor did it impose any sanction on it for failing to make adequate contributions. The company retained the right to amend the plan, in whole or in part, and was free to terminate the plan and distribute the trust assets (according to a schedule in the plan) at any time and for any reason. In sum, an employee who neither died, quit,

117

nor was discharged before age 65, *and who was "vested,"* would receive a pension if the company remained in business and elected to continue the plan in its existing form.

In April of 1974 Minnesota enacted the Private Pension Benefits Protection Act which had as one of its purposes the protection of employees of firms which went out of business. Under the law an employer who terminated a pension plan or closed its Minnesota office was required to pay a "pension funding charge," if the pension trust fund was insufficient to finance full pensions for *all* employees, regardless of whether they were "vested" or not, who had worked at least 10 years for the company. The "pension funding charge" took the form of a deferred annuity, payable to the employees at their normal retirement age.

After the enactment of the Act, Allied closed its Minnesota office and discharged all of its 30 employees. Nine of the discharged employees were not "vested," had no pension rights under the terms of the pension plan, but had worked for the company 10 or more years.

The Minnesota Act protected these nine employees, and in August of 1974 the state notified Allied that it owed a pension fund charge of $185,000 which would be used to assure that these nine employees would receive retirement benefits despite not having been vested in Allied's pension plan. Allied brought suit charging that the Act violated the contract clause of Article 1, § 10: "No State shall . . . pass any . . . Law impairing the Obligation of Contracts." The three-judge district court upheld the constitutional validity of the law, and Allied appealed to the Supreme Court.

Justice Stewart wrote the majority opinion in which Chief Justice Burger and Justices Powell, Rehnquist, and Stevens joined. Justice Brennan filed a dissenting opinion in which Justices White and Marshall joined. Justice Blackmun did not take part in the consideration or decision of the case.

THE MAJORITY OPINION

The almost complete text of the majority opinion is reprinted below. The roman numbers printed in **bold** type are not in the original opinion but are added to facilitate your relating the commentary, which follows, to specific passages in the opinion.

> [**I.**] There can be no question of the impact of the Minnesota Private Pension Benefits Protection Act upon the company's contractual relations with its employees. The Act substantially altered those relationships by superimposing pension obligations upon the company conspicuously beyond those that it had voluntarily agreed to undertake. But it does not inexorably follow that the Act, as applied to the company, violates the Contract Clause of the Constitution.
>
> The language of the Contract Clause appears unambiguously absolute. [Stewart quotes the clause here.] The Clause is not, however, the Draconian provision

that its words might seem to imply. As the Court has recognized, 'literalism in the construction of the contract clause . . . would make it destructive of the public interest by depriving the State of its prerogative of self-protection' [citation omitted].

Although it was perhaps the strongest single constitutional check on state legislation during our early years as a Nation [footnote omitted], the Contract Clause receded into comparative desuetude with the adoption of the Fourteenth Amendment, and particularly with the development of the large body of jurisprudence under the Due Process clause of that Amendment in modern constitutional history [footnote omitted]. Nonetheless, the Contract Clause remains part of the Constitution. It is not a dead letter. And its basic contours are brought into focus by several of this Court's 20th-century decisions.

[**II.**] First of all, it is to be accepted as a common place that the Contract Clause does not operate to obliterate the police power of the States. . . . 'One whose rights, such as they are, are subject to state restriction, cannot remove them from the power of the State, by making a contract about them. The contract will carry with it the infirmity of the subject matter'. . .

[**III.**] If the Contract Clause is to retain any meaning at all, however, it must be understood to impose some limits upon the power of a State to abridge existing contractual relationships, even in the exercise of its otherwise legitimate police power. The existence and nature of those limits were clearly indicated in a series of cases in this Court arising from the efforts of the State to deal with the unprecedented emergencies brought on by the severe economic depression of the early 1930's.

[**IV.**] In *Home Building & Loan Assn. v. Blaisdell*, 290 U.S. 398, the Court upheld against a Contract Clause attack a mortgage moratorium law that Minnesota had enacted to provide relief for homeowners threatened with foreclosure. Although the legislation conflicted directly with lenders' contractual foreclosure rights, the Court there acknowledged that, despite the Contract Clause, the States retain residual authority to enact laws 'to safeguard the vital interest of [their] people.' *Id.*, at 434. In upholding the state mortgage moratorium law, the Court found five factors significant. First, the state legislature had declared in the Act itself that an emergency need for the protection of homeowners existed. *Id.*, at 444. Second, the state law was enacted to protect a basic societal interest, not a favored group. *Id.*, at 445. Third, the relief was appropriately tailored to the emergency that it was designed to meet. *Ibid.* Fourth, the imposed conditions were reasonable. *Id.*, at 445-447. And, finally, the legislation was limited to the duration of the emergency. *Id.*, at 447.

The *Blaisdell* opinion thus clearly implied that if the Minnesota moratorium legislation had not possessed the characteristics attributed to it by the Court, it would have been invalid under the Contract Clause of the Constitution [footnote omitted]. These implications were given concrete force in three cases that followed closely in *Blaisdell*'s wake. (pp. 242-43)

[**V.**] In *W. B. Worthen Co. v. Thomas*, 292 U.S. 426, the court dealt with an Arkansas law that exempted the proceeds of a life insurance policy from collection by the beneficiary's judgment creditors. Stressing the retroactive effect of the state law, the Court held that it was invalid under the Contract

Clause, since it was not precisely and reasonably designed to meet a grave temporary emergency in the interest of the general welfare. In *W. B. Worthen Co. v. Kavanaugh*, 295 U.S. 56, the Court was confronted with another Arkansas law that diluted the rights and remedies of mortgage bondholders. The Court held the law invalid under the Contract Clause. 'Even when the public welfare is invoked as an excuse,' Mr. Justice Cardozo wrote for the Court, the security of a mortgage cannot be cut down 'without moderation or reason or in a spirit of oppression.' *Id.*, at 60. And finally, in *Treigle v. Acme Homestead Assn.*, 297 U.S. 189, the Court held invalid under the Contract Clause a Louisiana law that modified the existing withdrawal rights of the members of a building and loan association. 'Such an interference with the right of contract,' said the Court, 'cannot be justified by saying that in the public interest the operations of building associations may be controlled and regulated, or that in the same interest their charters may be amended.' *Id.*, at 196. . . . Despite the customary deference courts give to state laws directed to social and economic problems, '[l]egislation adjusting the rights and responsibilities of contracting parties must be upon reasonable conditions and of a character appropriate to the public purpose justifying its adoption' [*United States Trust Co. v. New Jersey*, 431 U.S. 1, 22 (1977)]. Evaluating with particular scrutiny a modification of a contract to which the State itself was a party, the Court in that case held that legislative alteration of the rights and remedies of Port Authority bondholders violated the Contract clause because the legislation was neither necessary nor reasonable. (p. 244)

[**VI.**] In applying these principles to the present case the first inquiry must be whether the state law has, in fact, operated as a substantial impairment of a contractual relationship.[16] The severity of the impairment measures the height of the hurdle the state legislation must clear. Minimal alteration of contractual obligations may end the inquiry at its first stage [footnote omitted]. Severe impairment, on the other hand, will push the inquiry to a careful examination of the nature and purpose of the state legislation.

[**VII.**] The severity of an impairment of contractual obligations can be measured by the factors that reflect the high value the Framers placed on the protection of private contracts. Contracts enable individuals to order their personal and business affairs according to their particular needs and interests. Once arranged, those rights and obligations are binding under the law, and the parties are entitled to rely on them. . . . [The opinion at this point reexamines the impact of the law upon Allied and concludes this review as follows.]

[**VIII.**] By simply proceeding to close its office in Minnesota, a move that had been planned before the passage of the Act, the company assessed an immediate pension funding charge of approximately $185,000.

---

[16]The novel construction of the Contract Clause expressed in the dissenting opinion is wholly contrary to the decisions of this Court. The narrow view that the Clause forbids only state laws that diminish the duties of a contractual obligor and not laws that increase them, a view arguably suggested by *Satterlee v. Matthewson*, 2 Pet. 380, has since been expressly repudiated. *Detroit United R. Co. v. Michigan*, 242 U.S. 238.

Thus, the statute in question nullifies express terms of the company's contractual obligations and imposes a completely unexpected liability in potentially disabling amounts. There is not even any provision for gradual applicability or grace periods [citations omitted].

[**IX.**] Yet there is no showing in the record before us that this severe disruption of contractual expectations was necessary to meet an important general social problem. The presumption favoring 'legislative judgment as to the necessity and reasonableness of a particular measure' [citation omitted] simply cannot stand in this case. . . .

[**X.**] [The legislation] has an extremely narrow focus. It applies only to private employers who have at least 100 employees, at least one of whom works in Minnesota, and who have established voluntary private pension plans . . . And it applies only when such an employer closes his Minnesota office or terminates his pension plan. Thus, this law can hardly be characterized, like the law at issue in the *Blaisdell* case, as one enacted to protect a broad societal interest rather than a narrow class [footnote omitted]. Moreover, in at least one other important respect the Act does not resemble the mortgage moratorium legislation whose constitutionality was upheld in the *Blaisdell* case. This legislation, imposing a sudden, totally unanticipated, and substantial retroactive obligation upon the company to its employees [footnote omitted] was not enacted to deal with a situation remotely approaching the broad and desperate emergency economic conditions of the early 1930's—conditions of which the Court in *Blaisdell* took judicial notice [footnote omitted].

[**XI.**] Entering a field it had never before sought to regulate, the Minnesota Legislature grossly distorted the company's existing contractual relationships with its employees by superimposing retroactive obligations upon the company substantially beyond the terms of its employment contracts. And that burden was imposed upon the company only because it closed its office in the state.

[**XII.**] This Minnesota law simply does not possess the attributes of those state laws that in the past have survived challenge under the Contract Clause of the Constitution. The law was not even purportedly enacted to deal with a broad, generalized economic or social problem. Cf. *Home Building & Loan Assn. v. Blaisdell*, 290 U.S., at 445. It did not operate in an area already subject to state regulation at the time the company's contractual obligations were originally undertaken, but invaded an area never before subject to regulation by the state. Cf. *Veix v. Sixth Ward Building & Loan Assn.*, 310 U.S. 32, 38 [footnote omitted]. It did not effect simply a temporary alteration of the contractual relationships of those within its coverage, but worked a severe, permanent, and immediate change in those relationships—irrevocably and retroactively. Cf. *United States Trust Co. v. New Jersey*, 341 U.S., at 22. And its narrow aim was leveled, not at every Minnesota employer, not even at every employer who left the State, but only at those who had in the past been sufficiently enlightened as voluntarily to agree to establish pension plans for their employees.

[**XIII.**] "Not Blaisdell's case, but Worthen's (*W. B. Worthen Co. v. Thomas*, [292 U.S. 426]) supplies the applicable rule" here. *W. B. Worthen Co. v. Kavanaugh*, 295 U.S., at 63. It is not necessary to hold that the Minnesota law impairs the obligation of the company's employment contracts "without moderation or reason in a spirit of oppression." *Id.*, at 60 [footnote omitted]. But we do hold that if the Contract Clause means anything at all, it means that Minnesota could not constitutionally do what it tried to do to the company in this case.

The judgment of the District Court is reversed.

COMMENTARY ON THE MAJORITY OPINION

Paragraph I. Justice Stewart begins by stressing the impact of the Act upon the contractual obligations Allied had with its employees—a theme he will return to later in the opinion. He then takes note of the constitutional *text* and the fact that the language of the text seems to bar *any* interference with contractual obligations. Yet he notes that *precedent* has recognized that the text is not to be read literally. In the next paragraph Stewart continues with a brief overview of the history of the contract clause.

Paragraph II. These passages raise a difficult problem, namely, how does the contract clause fit together with the "police power" of the state to regulate business. Using its police power, may a state willy-nilly interfere with any contract right, to any extent? Or does the contract clause block all state regulation of business when those regulations affect preexisting contractual arrangements? This portion of the opinion does not resolve these problems; it simply points to a tension between the police power and the contract clause.

Paragraph III. The opinion now begins to address the resolution of this tension.

Paragraph IV. In these passages Justice Stewart provides his analysis of precedent, and we can now begin to get a sense as to where Justice Stewart is headed in his opinion. He *narrowly* construes a precedent which had *upheld* a government policy affecting contract rights. By declaring certain facts as having been material to the decision in *Blaisdell*, Stewart narrows the occasion upon which interference with a contract would be permissible. In other words, Stewart pronounces that these factors were *sine qua non*—indispensable conditions—for the governmental policy to have been found constitutional. But note that in presenting his interpretation Stewart omits mention of the following sentence also found in *Blaisdell*: "Not only are existing laws read into contracts in order to fix obligations as between the parties, but the reservation of essential attributes of sovereign power is also read into contracts as a postulate of the legal order. . . ." That is, the *Blaisdell* opinion also said that every contract from its inception has automatically built into it the rule that the state may change the law whenever it suits itself to do so even if these changes affect the terms of the contract. Justice Stewart chooses to ignore this passage in order not to have it detract from his interpretation of *Blaisdell*.

Paragraph V. The next paragraphs of Stewart's opinion continue his examination of precedent. Stewart's brief review contains in somewhat disguised form various "tests" or "standards of review" that could be used to assess Minnesota's Private Pension Benefits Protection Act. From *Blaisdell* we learn that legislation affecting contract rights must meet certain criteria in order to be found constitutional. From *Thomas* we also learn that such legislation must be "precisely and reasonably designed to meet a grave temporary emergency." *Kavanaugh* lets us know such legislation must be passed with "moderation," with "reason," and not in a "spirit of oppression." *Treigle* warns that legislation affecting contracts cannot be justified by the vague claim that the law is "in the public interest." And *United States Trust* says such law "must be upon reasonable conditions," and, in addition, be "of a character appropriate to the public purpose justifying its adoption."

Now look what Stewart has done. He has hinted at the existence of various tests, standards of review, rules, principles, and doctrines with precedential value. More specifically, through this review of *precedent* Stewart has moved toward establishing the first or *legal premise* of his argument. That legal premise will be phrased in the form of a test, i.e., for legislation amending the terms of a contract that legislation must . . . etc. But we haven't yet gotten to the syllogism.

Paragraph VI. This is a remarkable paragraph. I'll "unpack" the paragraph, and then comment upon it. First, Stewart clearly assumes that his review of precedent has established certain "principles." Second, one of these principles seems to be the following: If the legislation made only a "minimal alteration of contractual obligations," then the case must end at this point; there would have been an insufficient injury to raise a constitutional question. He thus implies that legislatures may effect, through legislation, minimal alterations of contractual obligations; such minor alterations raise no constitutional question. If, third, the alteration is more than minimal then other principles come into play. These other principles hold that (1) the burden of proof is on the *state* to justify legislation which has more than a minimal impact on contract obligations; failure of the state to satisfy this burden of proof means the legislation will be struck down as unconstitutional; and (2) how heavy the state's burden of proof is varies depending upon how much the state's legislation impaired the contract. If the legislation "operated as a substantial impairment," then the state's burden will be heavier than if the impairment was modest. That is to say, the degree of care with which the Court will examine the legislation will vary depending on how far beyond "minimal" the impact is. Thus, Stewart adopts a *strategy of justification* that relies on *balancing* (see Chapter 4). That is, he says that the more severe the effect on a contract, the closer will be the scrutiny of the legislation, and the heavier the burden on the state. A severe impact, in order to be justified, must be balanced by governmental interests of great importance; i.e., severe impact can be balanced by sufficiently strong state interests.

Paragraph VI is also striking because it is not clearly linked to precedent. Justice Stewart's review of precedent does not demonstrate the existence of the framework he is now using. At most, that review suggests the existence of certain tests, and but hints that the burden of proof in these cases was on the state. In short, Stewart has used precedent in a creative manner to develop a new approach which is richer and more complex than that found in any explicit form in the precedent.

If you look back to paragraph VI you will see it includes footnote 16. In this footnote Justice Stewart dealt with several matters. He took on and rejected an argument made by the dissent that the contract clause does not apply to legislation which creates new obligations, as opposed to impairing preexisting contractual obligations. Justice Stewart argued that the precedent the dissent had relied on to make this argument had in fact been "repudiated" by the Court in subsequent cases. (I'll return to this point later.)

Stewart also took up in footnote 16 the question of the *original intent* of the framers. Again pointing to precedent, he said the Court had long ago rejected the view that the framers intended the clause only to apply to those laws which relieved debtors of their obligations to creditors.

Now let's anticipate where Justice Stewart is headed. Paragraph VI has set us up for the first major syllogism of his opinion. That syllogism, which is only *implied* in this paragraph, begins with this premise: (1A) It is legislation which has more than a minimal impact on contractual obligations which raises a constitutional issue. Given this premise, Stewart will now embark on an inquiry into the severity of the Minnesota law's impact on the contract between Allied and its employees.

Paragraph VII.   This paragraph, with its reference to the *intent of the framers*, clearly suggests that Justice Stewart is about to conclude that the Minnesota law had more than a "minimal" impact on the Allied contract. (In fact, there is a mini-argument buried in this paragraph. It goes like this: Because contract obligations are highly valued very few infringements of those obligations will be categorized as "minimal." This is so because we want to assure strong protection of the obligations of contract.) Stewart's reanalysis of the facts of the case leads him to the conclusion that the Minnesota law imposed a totally unexpected new, and expensive, obligation upon Allied. He stresses that the Act retroactively changed the employment compensation package between Allied and its employees, the terms of which Allied had relied on for many years.

Paragraph VIII.   Having reached this conclusion, Stewart has completed the first implicit syllogism of his opinion: (1A) *First Premise:* Legislation which has more than a minimal impact on contractual obligations raises a constitutional issue. (1B) *Second Premise:* This legislation has more than a minimal impact on contractual obligations. (1C) *Conclusion:* Therefore, this case does raise a constitutional issue under the contract clause.

At this point, according to the framework he outlined above, Stewart must select a test or standard of review to assess the constitutionality of the Minnesota law. He does this by simply announcing the test in the sentence immediately following Paragraph VIII.

Paragraph IX. Stewart's sentences compress a great deal of material into a small space. Implied in these sentences is his next important syllogism: (2A) *First Implicit Premise:* As our discussion of precedent has shown, laws which nullify express terms of contracts cannot be presumed to be constitutional, must be carefully examined, and must be justified by the state. According to the appropriate test, the state must prove that its law is "necessary to meet an important general social problem." (2B) *Second Premise* (explicitly established earlier in Paragraph VII): This law nullifies the terms of the Allied contract. (2C) *Implicit Conclusion:* In order for us to uphold the pension law, Minnesota must prove that this law is "necessary to meet an important general social problem."

In conclusion 2C Justice Stewart announces the test or standard of review he will use in this case. It is not clear where he got this test. If you look back at his review of the precedent (Paragraph V), you will not see any reference to this test. Stewart is thus, arguably, making new doctrine here by establishing a new test for resolving contract clause cases. This new approach is not compelled by the precedent, but it is not inconsistent with precedent. Finally, you should note that this test is a version of the "strict scrutiny" test (see Chapter 2).

This paragraph also contains, implicitly, yet one more syllogism. This syllogism begins with the implicit conclusion of the last syllogism: (3A) *First Implicit Premise:* In order for us to uphold the pension law, Minnesota must prove that this law is "necessary" to meet an important general social problem." (3B) *Second Premise* (explicitly stated above, but more fully supported later in the opinion): The state of Minnesota has not proved that its law is "necessary to meet an important general social problem." (3C) *Conclusion* (implicit here, but explicitly stated at the end of the opinion): The Minnesota law is unconstitutional.

Paragraph X. Stewart now takes up the question whether or not the state has met its burden of proof (i.e., whether the state's interests are strong enough to outweigh the impact on Allied's right). From *precedent* he draws, first, the principle that for the law to be justified it must protect a "broad societal interest" not a narrow class; he concludes that this law does not serve this kind of broad social interest. He also notes that precedent had only upheld legislation affecting contracts during a severe economic emergency. But, says Stewart, there is no such emergency here. Thus he *distinguishes* the *Blaisdell* case from this case on two grounds. Stewart has thus supported premise 3B.

(In footnote 24 of paragraph X Justice Stewart writes, "This is not to suggest that only an emergency of great magnitude can constitutionally justify a state law impairing the obligations of contracts." Stated differently, the existence of general economic depression is not a *sine qua non* of permissible state action affecting contract obligations. With this Stewart *broadens* his reading of *Blaisdell* beyond his earlier interpretation as discussed in Paragraph IV. If Stewart had now gone on to discuss exactly what other state interests would justify impairing contracts, such a discussion would have been *dictum*.

Paragraph XI. This paragraph serves several purposes. It once again restates the facts of the case in a way designed to make you believe in the injustice of what Minnesota has done. But the paragraph also sets the stage for the next paragraph in which Stewart applies the principles he earlier derived from precedent.

Paragraph XII. Stewart *distinguishes* the Minnesota case from precedent. While this discussion refers to several cases he has already discussed, this passage also mentions *Veix*, a case which Stewart had only briefly referred to in a footnote earlier in the opinion. In that footnote Stewart noted that *Veix* upheld a law because the petitioner had "purchased into an enterprise already regulated." Thus he *distinguishes Viex* from the Minnesota problem. And again Stewart has provided evidence in support of premise 3B.

Paragraph XIII. Once again Stewart seeks in this paragraph to limit the authority of the states to regulate business. He makes it clear that this law is being struck down despite the fact it was *not* passed "without moderation or reason or in a spirit of oppression." In other words, despite not being an extreme piece of legislation, this law is unconstitutional.

THE DISSENTING OPINION

I won't go through the dissenting opinion with the same thoroughness that I did the majority opinion. Instead I'll just summarize the argument of Justices Brennan, White, and Marshall. The opinion begins with an introductory section in which Justice Brennan asserts that the *text*, the *intent of the framers*, and *precedent* all support the conclusion that the contract clause prohibits only legislation which "diminished or nullified" a contract obligation due a person; it did not prohibit legislation which "while creating new duties, in nowise diminished the efficacy of any contractual obligation owed the constitutional claimant." The constitutionality of such legislation has, he says, always been adjudged under the due process clause of the Fourteenth Amendment. Brennan then notes that the majority's decision "greatly expands" the reach of the contract clause. The rest of Brennan's opinion elaborates on these points.

First he turns to his version of the facts of the case, a discussion which he uses to try to show you how reasonable Minnesota was in passing this law. The law, he notes, was designed to address a real social problem, namely, the protection of workers who, for various reasons, find that the pension plans they had counted on did not provide them with the support they expected. As for the economic impact of this law on employers, Justice Brennan notes that if employers had been adequately funding their pension plans all along, this law would have had only a minor economic impact on them. And, indeed, without this law, the employer who closes a plant would reap a "windfall" because he would *not* have to pay out a pension to those employees who had not vested in the plan. Finally, using an *analogy*, Justice Brennan says this law operates no differently than a law which requires employers to provide severance pay to employees when a plant closes.

In the next four pages of his opinion Justice Brennan seeks to demonstrate that this case should not be decided under the contract clause. He offers two reasons: (1) This law does not impair an obligation (it imposes a new obligation); and (2) the contract clause only deals with contract impairments. Sounding like an originalist, Justice Brennan argues that "the framers never contemplated that the Clause would limit the legislative power of States to enact laws creating duties that might burden some individual in order to benefit others." The contract clause was adopted, Brennan argues, mainly to stop legislatures from altering "obligations of contracts by effectively relieving one party of the obligation to perform a contract duty." Turning to the *text* of the clause, Justice Brennan stresses that the actual words of the Constitution speak in terms of "impairing" the obligations of contract. Now sounding like a literalist, Justice Brennan writes, "It is nothing less than an abuse of the English language to interpret, as does the Court, the term "impairing" as including laws which create new duties." Finally, concluding this section of his opinion, Justice Brennan cites a *precedent* which *upheld* a law which *gave validity* to a contract that otherwise would have been void. In that case the Court said, " 'But it surely cannot be contended, that to create a contract, and to destroy or impair one, means the same thing.' "

At this point in his opinion Brennan follows a *deductive* strategy of justification. His argument goes like this: *First Premise:* The text of the contract clause should be read literally. *Second Premise:* We must read the phrase "impairing the obligation of contracts" to mean diminish or damage preexisting contract obligations. Only laws which "impair" contract obligations are unconstitutional. *Third Premise:* This law does not diminish preexisting contract obligations; it imposes a new obligation on the employer. *Conclusion:* The Minnesota law does not violate the contract clause; in fact, the contract clause is irrelevant to deciding this case.

I want to interrupt the summary of Brennan's opinion here to stress how uncharacteristic a Brennan opinion this is. Justice Brennan is an advocate of noninterpretism, not an advocate of the strict adherence to a narrow view of the intent of the framers; nor has he been a literalist in the reading of the Constitution. In addition, Justice Brennan cites a precedent, *Satterlee v. Matthewson,* (1829), which yet other precedent has expressly rejected. In a footnote Justice Brennan gives the back of his hand to those cases. First he argues that those cases rested on a conservative view of government regulation which is now in disrepute. He then adds that the precedent which rejected *Satterlee* was "simply wrong."

Brennan's performance here is nothing less than remarkable. The precedents which rejected *Satterlee* have in fact never been overturned regarding their rejection of *Satterlee*. And Brennan expresses open contempt for the doctrine of precedent when he dismisses these precedents as "wrong," and, therefore, not to be followed.

The next major section of Brennan's opinion has five paragraphs mounting five distinct arguments.

- The contract clause does not protect all contract-based expectations as shown by the fact the contract clause does not apply to the impairment of contracts by the national government.
- The Court in prior cases has given states broad latitude "to effect even severe interference with existing economic values when reasonably necessary to promote the general welfare."
- Contract clause precedent has struck down legislation only when it "diluted with utter indifference to the legitimate interests of the beneficiary of a contract duty, the existing contract obligation. Brennan cites *W. B. Worthen Co. v. Kavanaugh* (1935) and *United States Trust Co. v. New Jersey* (1977).
- The tests and principles developed by the majority are too malleable and vague; they "vest judges with broad subjective discretion to protect property interests that happen to appeal to them." He illustrates this comment in a footnote by saying he cannot understand how the majority could assert that the Minnesota law did not deal with a broad, generalized social problem.
- The majority opinion is an "anomaly." Other precedent has permitted states to so regulate real property that its economic value was reduced by 90 percent. Relying on this *analogy*, Justice Brennan says there was no logical basis to permit this kind of regulation of real property and yet not uphold the pension law.

Justice Brennan begins the last section of his opinion by repeating his claim that the contract clause has no applicability to this case, and that the Act should be assessed under the due process clause of the Fourteenth Amendment. Thus he turns to a precedent decided under the Fourteenth Amendment, *Usery v. Turner Elkhorn Mining Co.* (1976). There the Court upheld a federal statute that required mine owners to compensate employees who had "contracted pneumoconiosis even though the employees had terminated their work . . . before the Act was passed. This federal statute imposed a new duty on operators based on past acts and applied even though the coal mine operators might not have known of the danger that their employees would contract pneumoconiosis at the time of the particular employees' service." Justice Brennan thus concludes that if the law in *Turner Elkhorn Mining* were constitutionally permissible, then the less oner- ous pension law, which also addresses a serious social problem, should also be upheld.

With this argument of Brennan we come to an important point about how methods of reasoning can be and are blended together. Brennan's argument combines the syllogism and the analogy. His argument goes like this: *First Premise* (implicit): Like cases should be decided alike. *Second Premise* (explic- it): *Turner Elkhorn Mining* and *Allied Structural Steel* are alike. *Conclusion:* Therefore, *Allied Structural Steel* should be decided the same and the Minnesota law upheld.

But note that hidden within this argument is an underlying justification based on the strategy of justification I called *balancing*. To see this you need to understand that the justification in *Turner Elkhorn Mining* was itself based on a test or standard of review that had the Court considering whether the social purposes of the law justified retroactive imposition of obligations on employers. Thus, when Justice Brennan uses this precedent in an argument based on analogy, he is *indirectly* adopting "balancing" as his mode of justification.

READING AND INTERPRETING SUPREME COURT OPINIONS

Briefing a Case

Look back now at the concluding section of Chapter 1 which reviews the basic features of a Supreme Court opinion. You should now be able to identify the facts of *Allied Structural Steel*, its procedural history, the legal claims, the issues, rulings, the reasoning of the majority opinion, and the holding. As a matter of fact, you should now be able to write a "brief" of this opinion (i.e., a summary of the opinion organized in terms of facts, procedural history, etc.). The brief could follow an outline something like this (different people set up their briefs differently):

1. Name of Case
2. Statement of Facts
3. Procedural History and Decision(s) in Lower Court(s)
4. Decision in Supreme Court
5. Statement of Issue(s)
6. Rulings on Each Issue
7. Justification Offered for Each Ruling
8. The Holding of the Case
9. Dissenting Opinion(s)

I won't write out an entire brief of the majority opinion, but I do want to comment on certain parts of the brief, beginning with the statement of issue(s). The issues of a case are those factual and/or legal questions regarding which parties to the case would answer differently. That is to say, these are the points of dispute. In this sense the basic legal issue of *Allied Structural Steel* could be phrased as follows: whether or not the Minnesota Private Pension Benefits Protection Act is constitutional. The problem with this formulation is that it does not convey enough information—it leaves out any reference to the specific section of the Constitution that may be involved in the case. And we know that this was an important problem in the case—was it the contract clause or the Fourteenth Amendment which was to be used in deciding the case?

Hence, version two of the issue might better look like this: whether or not the Minnesota Private Pension Benefits Protection Act violates the contract clause of Article I, § 10? Though this was the general, overriding issue in the case, as Justice Stewart structured his opinion, the case could be described as involving a set of narrower issues.

I will list those issues here, but not in the order in which they were taken up by Stewart. I do this to illustrate that when one summarizes an opinion one often takes up parts of an opinion in a different and, arguably, more logical order than they were taken up in the opinion itself. Remember, we are now looking at these opinions from the perspective of a reader trying to make our own sense of the opinion.

1. Does the contract clause apply to state legislation which amends a contractual relation by creating new duties, as opposed to diminishing existing contractual obligations?
2. Whether or not the Act operates as a substantial impairment of a contractual relationship?
3. Whether or not the Act was necessary to meet an important general social problem?

There are yet other matters that might have been listed as an issue (e.g., should strict scrutiny be used in assessing the constitutionality of a law which has a substantial effect upon a contractual relationship?). In any event, summarizing an opinion involves an act of judgment regarding what is the "best" version of the issues. One must decide whether to summarize the case in terms of one general issue, or in terms of multiple, smaller issues. You must decide which sequence is the most logical sequence in which to list the issues.

Justice Stewart reached a conclusion on each of three issues set out above. For example, as to the first issue, he "ruled" that the view that the contract clause forbids only state laws that diminish duties, and not laws that increase them, was expressly repudiated in precedent. He also reached conclusions on the other issues; you should be able to identify the rulings on the other issues. These conclusions are sometimes called "holdings," but to avoid confusing these "holdings" with "the holding" of the opinion I will call them "rulings."

Turning to the justifications for these rulings, you should be aware of the opinion's use of all the materials out of which a constitutional justification is built (e.g., text, intent of framers). Be sensitive to whether precedent was read broadly or narrowly. What analogies were used? Was precedent distinguished? What strategy of justification was used? What tests and standards of review were involved? What rules, principles, doctrines, tests, or standards of review may have precedential value? You may not include all this material in the brief, since the brief is intended to be brief.

Finally, let's turn to "the holding" of *Allied Structural Steel*. The holding might be stated as follows: It is a violation of the contract clause for a state retroactively to amend the employer-employee contract on pensions by imposing on the employer the new obligation of funding a pension for employees who worked for the employer for ten years but who were not vested in the plan according to the plan's terms for vesting. Given our discussion in this chapter, you should understand why this is a "narrow" formulation of the holding and why the following formulations are "broader."

Here are two somewhat broader versions. Alternatively, the holding might be stated as prohibiting a state from requiring a company to fund pensions that were not vested under the contract of employment. Phrased in yet more general terms, the holding might, arguably, have been said to prohibit a state from retroactively imposing almost any, more than minimal, new obligations on a party to a contract which modifies the terms of that contractual relationship.

Here is an extremely broad version of the holding: The contract clause prohibits both retroactive and prospective state regulation of all contractual relationships. This version is certainly too broad since *Allied Structural Steel* only involved the retroactive amendment of a preexisting contractual relationship.

Beyond the Brief

Briefs tend to be short summaries of an opinion, and because they are short much that could be said about the opinion is not included. For example, here are some additional questions about an opinion which you might not seek to answer in the writing of a brief:

- What strategy(ies) of justification were employed?
- What analogies were used in mounting the argument, and how were these analogies related to the strategies of justification?
- What exactly were the syllogisms implicitly or explicitly involved in building the argument, and how did these syllogisms relate to the strategy of justification, the analogies?

- What evidence was presented to prove the intent of the framers and the meaning of the text? or to establish claims made about "tradition," contemporary values, practical considerations?

When you start to answer such questions as these about an opinion, you take a first step toward the *critical* appraisal of the opinion, a first step toward deciding whether the opinion was well reasoned and whether or not the decision was correct in *your* opinion. In this connection you will want to ask these questions of the opinion:

- Are the premises of the opinion plausible and backed by evidence?
- Does the opinion argue logically from its premises? Are its logical deductions valid and is the overall opinion coherent?
- Has the opinion properly used or abused legal materials, e.g., text, evidence of original intent, evidence of tradition, considerations of prudence, precedent?
- Is the opinion rooted in a valid judicial philosophy?
- Does the opinion reflect acceptable fundamental principles?
- Has the Court announced rules, principles, and tests which are sufficiently clear and precise as to be enforceable and which do not leave the law in a state of uncertainty and confusion?

Interpreting the Opinion in Conjunction with Other Precedents

When you read an opinion, it will typically be but one opinion in a stream of opinions on the same general topic, some of which came before and some of which came after the opinion upon which you are concentrating. As a student of constitutional law your task is to locate the opinion with which you are concerned in the proper legal perspective. Thus you will need to ask such questions about the opinion (let's call it opinion M) as these:

- Did M provide a plausible interpretation of precedent, or did it abuse and misuse precedent?
- Did M overrule precedent?
- Did M reinterpret precedent and send constitutional law off in a new direction?
- Did M continue existing doctrine but carve out an "exception" to that doctrine?
- Is M simply inconsistent with precedent, leaving constitutional doctrine in a state of confusion and uncertainty?

- Is M but an aberration that will quickly be overruled, ignored, or modified?

The opinion in *Allied Structural Steel* raised many of these problems. As we saw, Justice Stewart narrowed the meaning of *Blaisdell*, thereby narrowing the occasion for *permissible* governmental limits on contractual obligations. That is, *Allied Structural Steel* seems to have reinvigorated the contract clause which, as Justice Stewart noted, had become virtually a dead letter in constitutional law. Stewart's opinion "expanded" the implications of the contract clause (i.e., narrowed the area of permissible state action, thereby expanding the number of policies that would probably be struck down as unconstitutional). Hence, we should ask whether this opinion represents the return of the conservative resistance to the regulation of business, a return to the period prior to the mid-1930s when the Court struck down one regulation after another.

But *Allied Structural Steel* may be an aberration. We know that in two subsequent cases the Court *upheld* state legislation which impaired contract obligations. In *Energy Reserves Group v. Kansas Power & Light Co.* (1983) the Court distinguished *Allied Structural Steel* by saying that the law in *Energy Reserves* was directed toward the entire natural gas industry and was not aimed at only a few firms. And in *Exxon Corp. v. Egerton* (1983) the Court upheld against a contract clause challenge a law imposing a heavy oil and gas severance tax. The law forbade producers from passing on the new tax burdens to consumers even though their sales contracts contained provisions allowing them to pass on tax increases to consumers. The Court, however, said the impact of the law on these preexisting contracts was only incidental.

What does all this mean? Can, on the one hand, *Energy Reserves* and *Exxon* and, on the other hand, *Allied Structural Steel* be reconciled so that *all* these cases remain "good law" and TOGETHER make up a coherent body of law? Or has *Allied Structural Steel* been effectively overruled, hence is no longer "good law"? In other words, have we changed direction again, modestly, or drastically? These are the kinds of questions you will be addressing regarding many sets of judicial opinions.

Let's now return to a question raised by Justice Brennan in his *Allied* dissent. What are we to make of the Supreme Court's direction when we take into account not just *Allied*, *Exxon*, and *Energy Reserves* but also (1) those many other Supreme Court opinions *upholding*, in the face of challenges under the Fourteenth Amendment, broad state authority to regulate business; and, (2) those many older and more recent opinions *upholding*, against challenges claiming an unlawful "taking," tough regulations on the use of real property? Against this background *Allied Structural Steel* truly looks like an anomaly. Or is it? There have been in very recent years cases which have, for example, struck down state controls on real property (*Nollan v. California Coastal Commission* [1987]). Hence, what we may see here is a still to be finally decided internal Court struggle between liberals and conservatives with the final victory yet to be won.

Going Deeper Still

Your analysis of a precedent can go yet farther and deeper. Here are some additional questions one might typically ask about an opinion.

- What judicial philosophy does the opinion reflect? Some version of interpretism or noninterpretism?
- Does this opinion reflect a version of conservatism or liberalism?
- What underlying moral value and/or political principles does the opinion embody and implicitly rest on?
- Which justices made up the majority and the dissenting positions? What does this tell us about who is in control of the Court?
- Was the opinion a bargained result? That is, is the opinion internally coherent or does it reflect uneasy compromise among justices with different views?

As for *Allied Structural Steel*, one could argue that it reflects an activist judicial philosophy, an activism on behalf of libertarian principles of free market capitalism. In resurrecting the contract clause the opinion arguably adopts the view that rights specifically mentioned in the Constitution should be vigorously protected by the judiciary. The opinion may thus represent a rejection of both the traditional ''conservative'' notion of judicial restraint which leaves standing legislation these justices personally believe is bad economic and social policy, and a rejection of the ''liberal'' position favoring legislative intervention into the economy for social welfare purposes.

The Larger Historical Picture

If one combines an examination of a single precedent with an analysis of its precedent, the cases which follow it, and other related constitutional developments, one starts to draw a bigger picture and to probe yet other themes. For example, here are some topics that might be explored in conjunction with such a wide-ranging examination of *Allied Structural Steel*.

- What theory of contracts and property rights does the Supreme Court embrace? What theory has it embraced in the past?
- Has the Court consistently supported capitalism? What version of capitalism?
- If there are inconsistencies among the opinions, what accounts for those inconsistencies?
  - —Is it simply a matter of changing political power on the American political stage?
  - —Are there basic inconsistencies and contradictions in American political culture which inevitably surface in Supreme Court opinions?

—Are these inconsistencies simply the accidental by-product of the collective decision-making process that takes place on the Court?
- What has been the Supreme Court's historical role in shaping American policy toward business and the economy?

One might begin to answer these questions by arguing that *Allied Structural Steel* adopts a "Lockean" or natural rights philosophy regarding property rights and freedom of contract. This political philosophy, one could continue, is affirmed by the Court as a way of imposing meaningful limits on the political process. Indeed, while government itself was established to limit the use of force and coercion and to protect liberty, this very instrument of social peace and tranquility can itself run amuck, and become the worst enemy of liberty. It was this danger that prompted the founders to establish a limited government, a government bound by a Constitution which imposes real constraints. Among the most important of those restraints are those to be found in the express protection the Constitution gives to property rights and contractual obligations. And, if these rights are to be effective in restraining the legislature, the Supreme Court must be active in its review and closely scrutinize legislation which affects those rights. It is this philosophy of government and judicial review which is arguably embodied in *Allied Structural Steel.*

We might continue our analysis by acknowledging that not all Supreme Court cases have reflected this political philosophy. Those other cases which permit government to regulate property and infringe contracts reflect another deep tradition in American culture—the tradition of communitarianism, the tradition of fraternalism. Thus we must conclude that American political culture reflects two sets of conflicting values, on the one hand, individualism, property rights, and freedom of contract, and on the other community, altruism, and fraternity. When these values come into conflict, sometimes one set attains dominance, and then the other. It is these deep tensions which show up in the Supreme Court's opinions and explain the inconsistent results.

The Court as Policymaker

Yet a different perspective one can take is to view the Supreme Court's opinions as exercises in policy-making, as the making of fundamental values and practical choices which shape the overall direction of governmental policy and the society. If you take this perspective on an opinion, you will be seeking to answer the following kinds of questions:

- What will be the political, social, and economic effects of the opinion? Were the effects of the decisions anticipated or unanticipated?
- Will the opinion have a differential effect on different groups of people?
- What is the Court's relationship with the other branches of government in the formulation of public policy?

- How much power does the Supreme Court have? Does its power vary from one policy arena to another?
- Have the Court's decisions changed society more than society changed the Court's decisions?

I won't attempt to answer all these questions regarding *Allied Structural Steel*, but it is interesting to note that the general practical implications of this opinion were probably negligible. Certainly Allied Structural Steel was itself saved from having to comply with the law. But beyond this, the striking down of the Minnesota law was of little social or economic significance. Why? Recall that the Minnesota law was adopted in April 1974. Shortly after its adoption Congress passed and the President signed a piece of federal legislation whose effective date was January 1, 1975. The Employee Retirement Insurance and Security Act explicitly preempts state laws from regulating private pension plans. Thus the Minnesota law was itself only in force less than nine months (April 1974 to January 1975), and today private pension funds are regulated by federal law.

Table of Cases

Index